LOW-CARB
MEDITERRANEAN
COOKBOOK

First Edition: 2023

Published by Mediterranean Nights

Printed in USA

Library of Congress Cataloging-in-Publication Data:

First edition.
Includes index.

Manufactured in USA

Introduction

A Hearty Welcome to Our Readers
Dear readers, it is with great pleasure that I extend a warm and heartfelt welcome to you as we embark on a culinary journey through the pages of this Low-Carb Mediterranean Cookbook. Within these recipes, you will find a delectable fusion of flavors, inspired by the rich culinary heritage of Europe, all carefully crafted to align with a low-carb lifestyle.

The Essence of Our Cookbook
The heart of this cookbook beats in harmony with the spirit of the Mediterranean diet, celebrated worldwide for its health benefits and delicious cuisine. In these pages, we will explore the marriage of European culinary traditions with the principles of low-carb eating, offering you a diverse array of dishes that are both nourishing and tantalizing to the taste buds.

Inspiration Behind the Cookbook
As the author of this cookbook, I have been profoundly inspired by the timeless wisdom of the Mediterranean way of life. The Mediterranean diet has long been associated with longevity, good health, and a profound appreciation for fresh, whole ingredients. My aim is to share this wisdom with you, offering a collection of recipes that can help you embrace the Mediterranean lifestyle while adhering to a low-carb regimen.

The Mediterranean region not only inspires us with its vibrant ingredients but also encourages a more relaxed and joyful approach to food. It's a place where meals are savored slowly, where good company is cherished, and where the pleasures of the table are an essential part of life. With this cookbook, I hope to bring a taste of this Mediterranean magic into your kitchen and onto your plates.

What Awaits Within

Within the pages of this cookbook, you will discover over 100 low-carb recipes that span the diverse landscapes of Europe. From the sun-kissed shores of Greece to the rustic villages of Italy, from the coastal elegance of France to the hearty traditions of Spain, our recipes will transport you to these enchanting regions. Each recipe has been thoughtfully crafted to embrace the Mediterranean's flavors, incorporating fresh vegetables, aromatic herbs, and the finest olive oils.

Whether you are seeking healthy and delicious meals to support your low-carb lifestyle, aiming to explore the captivating tastes of Europe, or simply looking to add new dimensions to your culinary repertoire, this cookbook has something special for you. So, join me in celebrating the harmony of Mediterranean and low-carb cooking, and let's embark on this flavorful journey together. Bon appétit!

Smoked Salmon and
Avocado Breakfast Bowl
See page, 4

The Heart and Soul of Mediterranean Low-Carb Cooking

In the pages of this cookbook, you will find that my approach to cooking and food is deeply rooted in the Mediterranean ethos, with a modern twist that embraces the principles of low-carb living. I believe that food should be a source of joy, nourishment, and vitality, and this philosophy underpins every recipe and technique presented here.

1. Freshness and Simplicity: At the core of Mediterranean cuisine lies the belief that the finest dishes are created from the freshest ingredients. I advocate for the use of seasonal produce, aromatic herbs, and high-quality olive oils. The recipes in this book are designed to let these ingredients shine, with a focus on simplicity and elegance.

2. Balancing Flavors: Mediterranean cooking is all about the harmonious blending of flavors. You will notice that our recipes are carefully crafted to strike a balance between the sweet and the savory, the tangy and the rich, creating a symphony of taste sensations on your palate.

3. Incorporating Lean Proteins: To adhere to a low-carb lifestyle, we prioritize lean sources of protein. You will find recipes featuring fish, poultry, and lean cuts of meat, all prepared in ways that preserve their natural flavors and textures.

4. Embracing Whole Grains: While we reduce overall carb content, we do acknowledge the value of whole grains. In some recipes, you will encounter whole grains like quinoa, farro, and barley, which add depth and nutrition to your meals.

5. Creative Use of Vegetables: Mediterranean cuisine celebrates the humble vegetable. Our recipes make vegetables the star of the show, whether roasted to perfection, incorporated into vibrant salads, or used to create hearty stews and casseroles.

6. Mediterranean Flavor Infusion: A hallmark of this cookbook is the infusion of Mediterranean flavors. Olive oil, garlic, lemon, and fresh herbs are used generously to transport you to the sun-soaked shores of the Mediterranean with every bite.

7. Mindful Eating: In keeping with Mediterranean traditions, we encourage mindful eating. Take time to savor each bite, enjoy meals with loved ones, and relish the experience of dining as a celebration of life.

8. Versatile Techniques: Our recipes encompass a range of cooking techniques, from grilling and roasting to simmering and braising. Each technique is selected to bring out the best in the ingredients, ensuring that your low-carb Mediterranean dishes are both delicious and nutritious.

9. Adaptability: I understand that dietary preferences and restrictions vary, so many recipes offer suggestions for customization. Whether you're vegetarian, pescatarian, or have other dietary needs, you can still enjoy the flavors of the Mediterranean while staying low-carb.

In essence, this cookbook is a celebration of the Mediterranean's culinary treasures, expertly adapted to cater to the health-conscious and those seeking delicious low-carb options. I invite you to embrace this approach to cooking, and I hope that these recipes inspire you to create meals that nourish your body and soul while delighting your taste buds with the timeless flavors of Europe.

**Smoked Salmon and
Avocado Breakfast Bowl**
See page, 40

Tips for Successful Cooking:

As you embark on your culinary journey through this cookbook, here are some valuable cooking tips and techniques that will enhance your experience and ensure your success in preparing these delightful low-carb Mediterranean dishes:

1. Knife Skills: A sharp knife is your best friend in the kitchen. Invest in a good-quality chef's knife and practice proper knife skills for efficient and safe food preparation. Precise chopping and slicing will make a difference in the presentation and texture of your dishes.

2. Seasoning: Seasoning is key to bringing out the flavors of your ingredients. Use sea salt and freshly ground black pepper liberally but mindfully. Taste as you go and adjust the seasoning to your liking.

3. Proper Searing: When searing meat or fish, ensure your pan is hot before adding the protein. This will help create a beautiful caramelized crust and seal in juices.

4. Roasting: Roasting vegetables or proteins is a common technique in Mediterranean cuisine. To achieve even browning, space out your ingredients on the baking sheet, and avoid overcrowding.

5. Grilling: Grilling imparts a wonderful smoky flavor to dishes. Preheat your grill, oil the grates, and ensure your ingredients are dry to prevent sticking. Use a meat thermometer for precise cooking temperatures.

6. Marinating: Marinating proteins like chicken or fish in Mediterranean-inspired mixtures of olive oil, garlic, herbs, and citrus enhances their flavor. Plan ahead, as marinating for at least 30 minutes (or longer) can make a significant difference.

7. Layering Flavors: Mediterranean cuisine often involves layering flavors. Start by sautéing aromatics like onions and garlic, then build your dish with herbs, spices, and liquids, allowing each layer to infuse the dish with depth.

8. Simmering and Braising: Low and slow cooking methods like simmering and braising are used for tenderizing tougher cuts of meat and creating rich, flavorful sauces. Patience is key here.

9. Embrace Fresh Herbs: Fresh herbs like basil, oregano, parsley, and mint are the stars of Mediterranean cooking. Add them toward the end of cooking for maximum flavor impact.

10. Balance Acids: Mediterranean cuisine often incorporates acidic elements like lemon juice and vinegar. Use them judiciously to balance flavors and brighten up dishes.

11. Fresh Ingredients: Whenever possible, opt for fresh, locally sourced, and seasonal ingredients. They are more flavorful and nutritious.

12. Quality Olive Oil: Invest in high-quality extra virgin olive oil for drizzling over salads, dipping bread, or finishing dishes. It's a hallmark of Mediterranean cooking.

13. Portion Control: Pay attention to portion sizes, especially if you're following a low-carb lifestyle. Mediterranean dishes are often served in smaller, balanced portions.

14. Wine Pairing: Don't forget to explore Mediterranean wine pairings. A crisp white wine or a bold red can elevate your dining experience.

15. Presentation: Take a moment to plate your dishes thoughtfully. Mediterranean cuisine is not only about taste but also about visual appeal. Garnish with fresh herbs, lemon wedges, or a drizzle of olive oil to add that final touch of elegance.

By mastering these cooking tips and techniques, you'll find yourself well-prepared to embark on a delicious and health-conscious culinary adventure through the pages of this cookbook. Remember, cooking is an art, and each dish is an opportunity to express your creativity and passion for food. Enjoy the journey!

Kitchen Essentials:

To ensure you have a smooth and enjoyable cooking experience while preparing the recipes in this cookbook, it's important to have the right kitchen tools and equipment at your disposal. Here is a list of essential kitchen tools and equipment that you'll frequently use, along with tips on how to use them effectively:

1. Chef's Knife: A good-quality chef's knife is indispensable. Keep it sharp and practice proper knife skills to make chopping, dicing, and slicing a breeze. Use a honing rod to maintain the blade's edge.

2. Cutting Board: Invest in a sturdy, non-slip cutting board to protect your countertops and ensure safe and efficient chopping and cutting.

3. Measuring Cups and Spoons: Accurate measurements are crucial in cooking. Use dry and liquid measuring cups as well as spoons for precise ingredient quantities.

4. Mixing Bowls: A set of mixing bowls in various sizes will come in handy for preparing ingredients, mixing sauces, and marinating proteins.

5. Whisk: A whisk is essential for blending and emulsifying ingredients, such as making vinaigrettes or beating eggs.

6. Skillet or Frying Pan: A good-quality skillet or frying pan is versatile and used for sautéing, searing, and frying. Ensure it's well-seasoned for non-stick cooking.

7. Saucepan: A saucepan is perfect for simmering sauces, soups, and grains. Opt for one with a heavy bottom for even heat distribution.

8. Baking Sheet: For roasting vegetables, baking fish, or toasting nuts and seeds. Line it with parchment paper for easy cleanup.

9. Grill: If you're into outdoor cooking, a grill is fantastic for achieving that smoky flavor in Mediterranean dishes. Ensure it's cleaned and oiled before grilling.

10. Food Processor or Blender: These are invaluable for making smooth sauces, dips, and dressings, as well as finely chopping nuts and herbs.

11. Mortar and Pestle: This traditional tool is great for grinding spices and making pesto or herb pastes, imparting a depth of flavor to your dishes.

12. Microplane Grater: Perfect for zesting citrus fruits and grating hard cheeses and spices like nutmeg.

13. Tongs: Invest in a good pair of tongs for flipping and turning foods while cooking, especially on the grill or in a skillet.

14. Colander: Used for draining pasta, washing vegetables, and straining liquids from cooked ingredients.

15. Oven Thermometer: To ensure your oven's temperature is accurate for baking and roasting.

16. Meat Thermometer: Essential for checking the internal temperature of meats to ensure they're cooked to perfection without overcooking.

17. Citrus Juicer: Extracting fresh juice from lemons and oranges is much easier with a citrus juicer.

18. Peeler: For quickly and safely peeling vegetables and fruits.

19. Silicone Spatula: Ideal for folding ingredients, scraping bowls, and ensuring you get every last bit of your delicious creations.

20. Timer: A kitchen timer will help you keep track of cooking times accurately, preventing overcooking or burning. with ease and confidence.

Mediterranean Turkey
and Avocado Salad
See page, 20

Tips on Using Kitchen Tools Effectively:

Keep Your Knives Sharp: A sharp knife is safer and more efficient. Regularly hone and sharpen your knives to maintain their edge.

Preheat Your Pans: Whether you're sautéing, searing, or roasting, always preheat your pans or ovens to the desired temperature before adding ingredients. This ensures even cooking.

Use Silicone Oven Mitts or Pot Holders: Protect your hands from burns when handling hot cookware or baking sheets.

Read the Recipe Thoroughly: Before you begin cooking, read the entire recipe to familiarize yourself with the steps and gather all the necessary tools and ingredients.

Clean as You Go: To keep your workspace organized and efficient, wash dishes, utensils, and cutting boards as you cook to minimize clutter.

Having these kitchen essentials and using them effectively will make your cooking experience enjoyable and allow you to create delicious, low-carb Mediterranean dishes

Flavor Pairing Suggestions:

One of the joys of cooking is the endless possibility for creativity, and Mediterranean cuisine offers a rich tapestry of flavors to explore. Here are some flavor pairing suggestions to inspire you and help you experiment with creating your own delightful recipes:

1. Tomato and Basil: The classic combination of ripe tomatoes and fresh basil is the essence of Mediterranean cuisine. Use them together in salads, pasta dishes, or atop grilled meats and fish.

2. Lemon and Garlic: The zesty brightness of lemon and the savory depth of garlic make for a dynamic duo. Combine them in marinades, salad dressings, or as a seasoning for roasted vegetables.

3. Olive Oil and Balsamic Vinegar: The luxurious richness of extra virgin olive oil pairs beautifully with the tangy sweetness of balsamic vinegar. Use this combination as a dipping sauce for bread or as a dressing for salads.

4. Mint and Lamb: The cool, refreshing taste of mint complements the robust flavor of lamb perfectly. Try it in Mediterranean-style meatballs, kebabs, or even a minty yogurt sauce.

5. Feta and Watermelon: The salty creaminess of feta cheese and the juicy sweetness of watermelon create a harmonious contrast. Combine them in salads with a drizzle of olive oil for a refreshing appetizer.

6. Cumin and Coriander: These warm, earthy spices are frequently used in Mediterranean cooking. They work wonders in spice rubs for meats, stews, and rice dishes.

7. Honey and Nuts: The natural sweetness of honey pairs wonderfully with the crunch of various nuts like almonds, walnuts, or pistachios. Use this combination to glaze roasted vegetables or drizzle over yogurt.

8. Saffron and Seafood: The delicate aroma and golden hue of saffron elevate seafood dishes. Use it in paella, risotto, or a fragrant seafood broth.

9. Garlic and Rosemary: The pungent kick of garlic and the fragrant, woody notes of rosemary are a match made in culinary heaven. Use them to season roasted potatoes, grilled chicken, or lamb.

10. Olives and Citrus: The briny, salty flavor of olives pairs beautifully with the bright acidity of citrus fruits like oranges or lemons. Try them together in salads or as a garnish for fish dishes.

11. Yogurt and Cucumber: The creamy tanginess of yogurt and the crisp freshness of cucumber are the basis of tzatziki, a popular Mediterranean dip. Use it as a condiment or dip for grilled meats and vegetables.

12. Paprika and Garlic: Smoked or sweet paprika adds depth and smokiness, while garlic provides a pungent kick. Combine them to season roasted chicken, grilled shrimp, or vegetable skewers

Table of Contents

Chapter 1: Mediterranean Mornings with Few Carbs, 1
Greek Omelette with Spinach and Feta, 2
Mediterranean Scrambled Eggs with Olives, 3
Smoked Salmon and Avocado Breakfast Bowl, 4
Veggie-Packed Mediterranean Breakfast Casserole, 5
Low-Carb Greek Yogurt Parfait, 6
Mediterranean Shakshuka with Zucchini Noodles, 7
Greek-style Breakfast Wrap with Lettuce, 8
Tomato and Cucumber Breakfast Salad, 9
Keto Mediterranean Quiche, 10
Mediterranean Egg Muffins with Sun-Dried Tomatoes, 11
Chapter 2: Low-Carb Mediterranean Lunches, 12
Greek Salad with Grilled Chicken Breast, 13
Mediterranean Tuna Salad Lettuce Wraps, 14
Zucchini and Feta Stuffed Peppers, 15
Keto Greek Chicken and Veggie Skewers, 16
Mediterranean Cauliflower Rice Bowl, 17
Low-Carb Greek Cucumber and Yogurt Soup, 18
Italian Roasted Veggie Salad with Pesto, 19
Mediterranean Turkey and Avocado Salad, 20
Mediterranean Stuffed Bell Peppers (Low-Carb), 21
Greek-style Chicken and Spinach Salad, 22
Chapter 3: Dinner Delights, Few Carbs, 23
Baked Salmon with Lemon and Dill, 24
Greek-Style Grilled Swordfish, 25
Garlic Shrimp with Roasted Asparagus, 26
Mediterranean Chicken Thighs with Olives, 27
Keto Eggplant Parmesan, 28
Lemon Herb Baked Cod with Vegetables, 29
Mediterranean Lamb Chops with Tzatziki, 30
Italian Stuffed Portobello Mushrooms, 31
Low-Carb Mediterranean Beef Stir-Fry, 32
Lemon and Garlic Grilled Zucchini, 33
Chapter 4: Low-Carb Mediterranean Vegetable Sides, 34
Greek-Style Roasted Cauliflower, 35
Mediterranean Grilled Eggplant, 36
Lemon and Garlic Roasted Brussels Sprouts, 37
Greek Zucchini Fritters, 38
Mediterranean Broccoli Salad, 39
Italian Baked Parmesan Tomatoes, 40
Roasted Asparagus with Feta and Lemon, 41
Low-Carb Mediterranean Cucumber Salad, 42
Lemon and Herb Roasted Artichokes, 43
Mediterranean Spaghetti Squash, 44
We have a small favor to ask, 45
Chapter 5: Sweet and Low-Carb Mediterranean Endings, 46
Greek Yogurt with Berries and Nuts, 47
Dark Chocolate-Dipped Strawberries, 48
Almond and Orange Blossom Ricotta Tart, 49
Low-Carb Mediterranean Almond Cookies, 50
Lemon Sorbet with Fresh Mint, 51
Mediterranean Chia Seed Pudding, 52
Greek Yogurt Cheesecake Bites, 53
Keto Baklava with Almonds and Walnuts, 54
Low-Carb Mediterranean Berry Parfait, 55
Almond and Orange Blossom Semolina Cake (Low-Carb), 56
Chapter 6: Low-Carb Mediterranean Seafood Delights, 57
Mediterranean Shrimp Scampi, 58
Grilled Octopus with Lemon and Herbs, 59
Baked Trout with Mediterranean Salsa, 60
Lemon and Herb Seared Scallops, 61
Keto Mediterranean Tuna Steak, 62
Mediterranean Salmon Cakes, 63
Garlic Butter Lobster Tails, 64
Greek-Style Grilled Sardines, 65
Lemon and Herb Swordfish Skewers, 66
Low-Carb Mediterranean Seafood Stew, 67

Chapter 7: Lean and Low-Carb Mediterranean Meats, 68
Mediterranean Pork Tenderloin with Olive Tapenade, 69
Italian Balsamic Glazed Chicken Thighs, 70
Keto Greek Lamb Kebabs, 71
Low-Carb Mediterranean Beef Kofta, 72
Garlic and Herb Marinated Chicken Breasts, 73
Mediterranean Turkey and Spinach Stuffed Mushrooms, 74
Lemon and Herb Grilled Veal Chops, 75
Mediterranean Meatloaf with Feta, 76
Greek-Style Beef and Eggplant Skillet, 77
Low-Carb Moroccan Spiced Lamb Chops, 78
Chapter 8: Low-Carb Sides and Salads for Mediterranean Dining, 79
Mediterranean Roasted Radishes, 80
Greek-Style Grilled Zucchini, 81
Lemon and Garlic Sauteed Spinach, 82
Italian Grilled Eggplant with Pesto, 83
Mediterranean Cucumber and Feta Salad, 84
Low-Carb Roasted Artichokes, 85
Greek-Style Cauliflower Rice Pilaf, 86
Mediterranean Brussels Sprouts with Pancetta, 87
Low-Carb Italian Caprese Salad, 88
Lemon and Herb Grilled Portobello Mushrooms, 89
Chapter 9: Low-Carb Mediterranean Pasta Alternatives, 90
Zucchini Noodles with Pesto and Tomatoes, 91
Mediterranean Spaghetti Squash with Olives, 92
Greek-Style Cabbage Noodles with Feta, 93
Low-Carb Eggplant "Lasagna", 94
Italian Riced Cauliflower Risotto, 95
Lemon and Garlic Sautéed Broccoli Rabe, 96
Mediterranean Cabbage and Beef Stir-Fry, 97
Low-Carb Greek Zoodle Salad, 98
Mediterranean Green Bean "Pasta", 99
Italian Baked Parmesan Zucchini, 100
Chapter 10: Low-Carb Mediterranean Sweet Treats, 101
Greek Yogurt with Berries and Almonds, 102
Low-Carb Dark Chocolate Bark with Nuts, 103
Almond and Coconut Flour Pancakes, 104
Lemon and Almond Flour Cake, 105
Mediterranean Avocado Chocolate Mousse, 106
Keto Panna Cotta with Berry Compote, 107
Greek Yogurt Cheesecake Muffins, 108
Low-Carb Mediterranean Almond Biscotti, 109
Lemon and Almond Ricotta Muffins, 110
Italian Low-Carb Tiramisu, 111
Chapter 11: Low-Carb Mediterranean Vegan Delights, 112
Mediterranean Vegan Chickpea Salad, 113
Italian Vegan Zucchini Noodles with Pesto, 114
Low-Carb Mediterranean Stuffed Bell Peppers (Vegan), 115
Greek-Style Vegan Moussaka, 116
Mediterranean Vegan Tofu Stir-Fry, 117
Vegan Italian Eggplant Parmesan, 118
Low-Carb Mediterranean Vegan Lentil Soup, 119
Vegan Mediterranean Cabbage Rolls, 120
Italian Vegan Caprese Salad, 121
Mediterranean Vegan Spaghetti Squash, 122
We have a small favor to ask, 123

Chapter 1:
Mediterranean Mornings with Few Carbs

1 omelette   280   15

Greek Omelette with Spinach and Feta

Dive into the heart of Greece with this savory omelette, brimming with spinach and creamy feta. A morning delight that's rich in flavor and low in carbs.
Originating from the sunny shores of Crete, this dish has been cherished for generations for its simplicity and healthfulness.

Ingredients:

- 2 large eggs
- 1/2 cup fresh spinach, chopped
- 1/4 cup crumbled feta cheese
- 1/4 teaspoon dried oregano
- Salt and pepper to taste

Directions

1. In a bowl, whisk eggs, oregano, salt, and pepper.
2. Heat a non-stick skillet over medium-high heat.
3. Add spinach and sauté until wilted.
4. Pour egg mixture over spinach.
5. Sprinkle feta on top. Cook until set.
6. Fold in half and serve. Enjoy your Greek omelette!

1 serving   220   10

Mediterranean Scrambled Eggs with Olives

Take your taste buds on a journey to the Mediterranean coast with these flavorful scrambled eggs featuring the briny goodness of olives.
A dish inspired by lazy mornings in Greek villages, where life is simple and flavors are robust.

Ingredients:

- 2 large eggs
- 6 pitted Kalamata olives, chopped
- 1 tablespoon olive oil
- 1 tablespoon fresh parsley, chopped
- Salt and pepper to taste

Directions

1. In a bowl, whisk eggs, salt, and pepper.
2. Heat olive oil in a pan over medium heat.
3. Add olives and sauté briefly.
4. Pour in whisked eggs.
5. Scramble until cooked to your liking.
6. Garnish with fresh parsley. Serve and savor the Mediterranean flavors.

1 bowl | 320 | 10

Smoked Salmon and Avocado Breakfast Bowl

Delight in a refreshing morning bowl of smoked salmon and creamy avocado, reminiscent of coastal Mediterranean mornings.
A popular choice along the shores of the French Riviera, where freshness meets indulgence.

Ingredients:

- 2 oz smoked salmon
- 1/2 avocado, sliced
- 1/4 cup cherry tomatoes, halved
- 2 tablespoons red onion, finely chopped
- 1 tablespoon capers
- Lemon wedges for garnish

Directions

1. Arrange smoked salmon, avocado, cherry tomatoes, and red onion in a bowl.
2. Sprinkle capers on top.
3. Serve with lemon wedges.
4. Enjoy your Mediterranean breakfast bowl bursting with flavors.

1 serving — 280 kcal — 30

Veggie-Packed Mediterranean Breakfast Casserole

Indulge in a wholesome breakfast casserole packed with Mediterranean goodness. A dish inspired by the vibrant markets of Istanbul, where flavors collide.

Ingredients:

- 2 large eggs
- 1/4 cup bell peppers, diced
- 1/4 cup cherry tomatoes, halved
- 1/4 cup baby spinach, chopped
- 1/4 cup feta cheese, crumbled
- 1/4 teaspoon dried oregano
- Salt and pepper to taste

Directions

1. Preheat your oven to 350°F (175°C).
2. In a bowl, whisk eggs, oregano, salt, and pepper.
3. Grease a baking dish.
4. Layer bell peppers, cherry tomatoes, and spinach.
5. Pour the egg mixture over.
6. Sprinkle with feta. Bake for 20-25 minutes.
7. Serve warm. A taste of Istanbul on your plate!

1 parfait 180 5

Low-Carb Greek Yogurt Parfait

Start your day with a guilt-free delight - a Greek yogurt parfait bursting with flavors. Inspired by the ancient Greek practice of enjoying yogurt with honey and fruits for vitality.

Ingredients:

- 1/2 cup Greek yogurt
- 1/4 cup fresh berries (blueberries, strawberries)
- 1 tablespoon honey
- 1 tablespoon chopped nuts (walnuts or almonds)

Directions

1. In a glass, layer yogurt, berries, and honey.
2. Repeat until the glass is filled.
3. Top with chopped nuts.
4. Drizzle extra honey if desired.
5. Savor the ancient goodness of Greek yogurt parfait.

1 serving   320   20

Mediterranean Shakshuka with Zucchini Noodles

Ingredients:

- 2 large eggs
- 1 zucchini, spiralized into noodles
- 1/2 cup tomato sauce
- 1/4 cup bell peppers, diced
- 1/4 teaspoon ground cumin
- Salt and pepper to taste

Dive into a flavorful Mediterranean breakfast with a twist - shakshuka with zucchini noodles. A dish inspired by the bustling markets of Tel Aviv, where spices dance in harmony.

Directions

1. In a skillet, heat tomato sauce and bell peppers.
2. Add cumin, salt, and pepper.
3. Make wells in the sauce and crack eggs into them.
4. Cover and cook until eggs are set.
5. In a separate pan, sauté zucchini noodles until tender.
6. Serve eggs on zucchini noodles. Enjoy the Tel Aviv-inspired shakshuka!

1 wrap   260   15

Greek-style Breakfast Wrap with Lettuce

Embrace the Greek flavors wrapped in a lettuce leaf with this morning delight. Inspired by the streets of Athens, where handheld breakfasts are a tradition.

Ingredients:

- 2 large eggs, scrambled
- 2 slices of ham
- 1/4 cup cherry tomatoes, halved
- 1/4 cup cucumber, sliced
- 2 large lettuce leaves
- Tzatziki sauce for drizzling

Directions

1. Place scrambled eggs on a lettuce leaf.
2. Top with ham, tomatoes, and cucumber.
3. Drizzle with tzatziki sauce.
4. Wrap and enjoy your Athenian breakfast delight.

1 serving   120   10

Tomato and Cucumber Breakfast Salad

Start your day with a refreshing Mediterranean breakfast salad, inspired by the sunny fields of Spain.
A delightful blend of flavors and textures.

Ingredients:

- 1 cup cherry tomatoes, halved
- 1/2 cucumber, sliced
- 1/4 cup red onion, thinly sliced
- 2 tablespoons fresh basil, chopped
- 1 tablespoon olive oil
- 1 tablespoon balsamic vinegar
- Salt and pepper to taste

Directions

1. In a bowl, combine tomatoes, cucumber, and red onion.
2. Drizzle with olive oil and balsamic vinegar.
3. Add basil, salt, and pepper.
4. Toss gently.
5. Enjoy the taste of sunny Spain in your breakfast salad.

1 slice | 280 | 45

Keto Mediterranean Quiche

Savor a slice of Mediterranean heaven with this keto-friendly quiche.
A recipe passed down through generations in the coastal villages of Italy, where love for food knows no bounds.

Ingredients:

- 1 almond flour pie crust
- 3 large eggs
- 1/2 cup heavy cream
- 1/4 cup black olives, sliced
- 1/4 cup roasted red peppers, chopped
- 1/4 cup feta cheese, crumbled
- 1/4 teaspoon dried basil
- Salt and pepper to taste

Directions

1. Preheat your oven to 350°F (175°C).
2. In a bowl, whisk eggs and heavy cream.
3. Add olives, roasted red peppers, feta, basil, salt, and pepper.
4. Pour into the pie crust.
5. Bake for 35-40 minutes.
6. Allow to cool before slicing.
7. Enjoy a slice of coastal Italy with your keto Mediterranean quiche.

1 muffin   150   25

Mediterranean Egg Muffins with Sun-Dried Tomatoes

These Mediterranean egg muffins with sun-dried tomatoes are a perfect grab-and-go breakfast.
Inspired by the rustic charm of Greek villages, where homemade flavors reign supreme.

Ingredients:

- 4 large eggs
- 1/4 cup sun-dried tomatoes, chopped
- 1/4 cup baby spinach, chopped
- 1/4 cup feta cheese, crumbled
- 1/4 teaspoon dried oregano
- Salt and pepper to taste

Directions

1. Preheat your oven to 350°F (175°C) and grease a muffin tin.
2. In a bowl, whisk eggs, oregano, salt, and pepper.
3. Stir in sun-dried tomatoes, spinach, and feta.
4. Pour into muffin cups.
5. Bake for 20-25 minutes.
6. Enjoy these homemade Mediterranean egg muffins.

Chapter 2:
Low-Carb
Mediterranean Lunches

1 serving | 350 | 20

Greek Salad with Grilled Chicken Breast

Enjoy the classic flavors of Greece in a hearty salad with grilled chicken breast.
A salad inspired by the vibrant street markets of Athens.

Ingredients:

- 4 oz boneless, skinless chicken breast
- 2 cups mixed greens
- 1/4 cup cherry tomatoes, halved
- 1/4 cup cucumber, sliced
- 1/4 cup Kalamata olives, pitted
- 1/4 cup red onion, thinly sliced
- 1/4 cup feta cheese, crumbled
- 2 tablespoons extra-virgin olive oil
- 1 tablespoon red wine vinegar
- 1 teaspoon dried oregano
- Salt and black pepper to taste

Directions

1. Season chicken breast with salt, pepper, and olive oil. Grill until cooked through, about 6-8 minutes per side. Slice.
2. In a large bowl, combine mixed greens, cherry tomatoes, cucumber, Kalamata olives, red onion, and feta cheese.
3. In a separate bowl, whisk together olive oil, red wine vinegar, dried oregano, salt, and pepper to make the dressing.
4. Drizzle the dressing over the salad and toss.
5. Top with grilled chicken slices.
6. Enjoy your taste of Athens with Greek salad and grilled chicken.

2 wraps   **220**   **15**

Mediterranean Tuna Salad Lettuce Wraps

Delight in a light and refreshing Mediterranean tuna salad wrapped in lettuce leaves.
A dish that echoes the coastal breeze of the Mediterranean.

Ingredients:

- 1 can (5 oz) tuna in water, drained
- 1/4 cup cucumber, diced
- 1/4 cup cherry tomatoes, diced
- 1/4 cup red bell pepper, diced
- 2 tablespoons red onion, finely chopped
- 2 tablespoons Kalamata olives, pitted and chopped
- 2 tablespoons fresh parsley, chopped
- 1 tablespoon lemon juice
- 2 tablespoons Greek yogurt
- Salt and black pepper to taste

Directions

1. In a bowl, combine tuna, cucumber, cherry tomatoes, red bell pepper, red onion, Kalamata olives, and fresh parsley.
2. In a separate bowl, whisk together lemon juice, Greek yogurt, salt, and pepper to make the dressing.
3. Pour the dressing over the tuna salad and toss to coat.
4. Spoon the tuna salad into lettuce leaves and wrap them up.
5. Enjoy your Mediterranean tuna salad lettuce wraps.

1 pepper | 280 | 40

Zucchini and Feta Stuffed Peppers

Explore the fusion of flavors in zucchini and feta stuffed peppers, a low-carb Mediterranean delight.
A dish inspired by the creative kitchens of Crete.

Ingredients:

- 1 large bell pepper
- 1 small zucchini, diced
- 1/4 cup red onion, finely chopped
- 1/4 cup crumbled feta cheese
- 2 tablespoons fresh dill, chopped
- 1 clove garlic, minced
- 1 tablespoon olive oil
- Salt and black pepper to taste

Directions

1. Preheat your oven to 375°F (190°C).
2. Slice the top off the bell pepper and remove the seeds.
3. In a skillet, heat olive oil and sauté zucchini, red onion, and garlic until tender.
4. Remove from heat and stir in crumbled feta and fresh dill. Season with salt and pepper.
5. Stuff the bell pepper with the zucchini and feta mixture.
6. Place the stuffed pepper in a baking dish and bake for 30-35 minutes until the pepper is tender.
7. Enjoy your zucchini and feta stuffed pepper, a taste of Crete on your plate.

1 serving   340   30

Keto Greek Chicken and Veggie Skewers

Indulge in the flavors of the Mediterranean with Keto Greek chicken and veggie skewers, grilled to perfection.
A dish inspired by the seaside tavernas of Santorini.

Ingredients:

- 4 oz boneless, skinless chicken breast, cut into cubes
- 1/2 cup bell peppers, diced
- 1/2 cup zucchini, sliced
- 1/4 cup red onion, diced
- 1/4 cup cherry tomatoes
- 2 tablespoons olive oil
- 1 tablespoon fresh lemon juice
- 1 teaspoon dried oregano
- Salt and black pepper to taste

Directions

1. In a bowl, combine chicken cubes, bell peppers, zucchini, red onion, and cherry tomatoes.
2. In a separate bowl, whisk together olive oil, lemon juice, dried oregano, salt, and pepper to make the marinade.
3. Pour the marinade over the chicken and vegetable mixture.
4. Thread the chicken and veggies onto skewers.
5. Preheat your grill to medium-high heat.
6. Grill the skewers for 10-12 minutes, turning occasionally, until the chicken is cooked through and veggies are tender.
7. Enjoy your Keto Greek chicken and veggie skewers, a taste of Santorini.

1 serving | 260 | 20

Mediterranean Cauliflower Rice Bowl

Immerse yourself in the wholesome goodness of a Mediterranean cauliflower rice bowl.
A dish inspired by the fertile fields of Cyprus.

Ingredients:

- 1 cup cauliflower rice
- 4 oz grilled chicken breast, sliced
- 1/4 cup cucumber, diced
- 1/4 cup cherry tomatoes, halved
- 1/4 cup Kalamata olives, pitted and sliced
- 2 tablespoons red onion, finely chopped
- 2 tablespoons feta cheese, crumbled
- 2 tablespoons fresh parsley, chopped
- 1 tablespoon extra-virgin olive oil
- 1 tablespoon lemon juice
- Salt and black pepper to taste

Directions

1. In a bowl, combine cauliflower rice, grilled chicken slices, cucumber, cherry tomatoes, Kalamata olives, red onion, feta cheese, and fresh parsley.
2. In a separate bowl, whisk together olive oil, lemon juice, salt, and pepper to make the dressing.
3. Drizzle the dressing over the cauliflower rice bowl and toss to combine.
4. Enjoy your Mediterranean cauliflower rice bowl, a taste of Cyprus on your plate.

1 serving   180   15

Low-Carb Greek Cucumber and Yogurt Soup

Savor the cool and creamy delight of low-carb Greek cucumber and yogurt soup.
A soup that echoes the breezy islands of the Aegean.

Ingredients:

- 1 cucumber, peeled and diced
- 1 cup Greek yogurt
- 1/4 cup fresh dill, chopped
- 1 clove garlic, minced
- 1 tablespoon extra-virgin olive oil
- 1 tablespoon lemon juice
- Salt and black pepper to taste

Directions

1. In a blender, combine diced cucumber, Greek yogurt, fresh dill, minced garlic, olive oil, lemon juice, salt, and pepper.
2. Blend until smooth.
3. Chill the soup in the refrigerator for at least 1 hour before serving.
4. Stir before serving, and garnish with additional fresh dill if desired.
5. Enjoy your low-carb Greek cucumber and yogurt soup, a taste of the Aegean islands.

1 serving | 280 | 30

Italian Roasted Veggie Salad with Pesto

Dive into the vibrant flavors of an Italian roasted veggie salad with pesto dressing. A salad inspired by the open-air markets of Florence.

Ingredients:

- 2 cups mixed roasted vegetables (bell peppers, zucchini, cherry tomatoes)
- 2 cups mixed greens
- 2 tablespoons pesto sauce
- 1 tablespoon balsamic vinegar
- 1 tablespoon extra-virgin olive oil
- 1/4 cup Parmesan cheese shavings
- Salt and black pepper to taste

Directions

1. Toss mixed roasted vegetables with pesto sauce, balsamic vinegar, and olive oil.
2. In a large bowl, place mixed greens.
3. Top with the dressed roasted vegetables.
4. Garnish with Parmesan cheese shavings.
5. Season with salt and pepper to taste.
6. Enjoy your Italian roasted veggie salad with pesto, a taste of Florence.

1 serving — 340 — 20

Mediterranean Turkey and Avocado Salad

Indulge in a satisfying Mediterranean turkey and avocado salad with a zesty lemon dressing.
A salad inspired by the markets of Istanbul.

Ingredients:

- 4 oz turkey breast slices
- 1/2 avocado, sliced
- 2 cups mixed greens
- 1/4 cup cherry tomatoes, halved
- 1/4 cup cucumber, sliced
- 2 tablespoons red onion, finely chopped
- 1 tablespoon fresh mint, chopped
- 1 tablespoon fresh parsley, chopped
- 1 tablespoon extra-virgin olive oil
- 1 tablespoon lemon juice
- Salt and black pepper to taste

Directions

1. In a large bowl, combine turkey breast slices, avocado slices, mixed greens, cherry tomatoes, cucumber, red onion, fresh mint, and fresh parsley.
2. In a separate bowl, whisk together olive oil, lemon juice, salt, and pepper to make the dressing.
3. Drizzle the dressing over the salad and toss.
4. Enjoy your Mediterranean turkey and avocado salad, a taste of Istanbul.

1 pepper | 320 | 45

Mediterranean Stuffed Bell Peppers (Low-Carb)

Savor the flavors of the Mediterranean with low-carb stuffed bell peppers, brimming with wholesome ingredients.
A dish inspired by the home-cooked meals of Mykonos.

Ingredients:

- 1 large bell pepper
- 1/4 cup ground turkey
- 1/4 cup cauliflower rice
- 1/4 cup cherry tomatoes, diced
- 2 tablespoons red onion, finely chopped
- 2 tablespoons Kalamata olives, pitted and chopped
- 2 tablespoons fresh parsley, chopped
- 1 clove garlic, minced
- 1 tablespoon extra-virgin olive oil
- Salt and black pepper to taste

Directions

1. Preheat your oven to 375°F (190°C).
2. Slice the top off the bell pepper and remove the seeds.
3. In a skillet, heat olive oil and sauté ground turkey, cauliflower rice, cherry tomatoes, red onion, Kalamata olives, and minced garlic until turkey is cooked through. Season with salt and pepper.
4. Stuff the bell pepper with the turkey and cauliflower mixture.
5. Place the stuffed pepper in a baking dish and bake for 30-35 minutes until the pepper is tender.
6. Enjoy your Mediterranean stuffed bell pepper, a taste of Mykonos on your plate.

1 serving   320   25

Greek-style Chicken and Spinach Salad

Relish the Greek flavors in a chicken and spinach salad with a tangy yogurt dressing. A salad inspired by the seaside tavernas of Rhodes.

Ingredients:

- 4 oz grilled chicken breast, sliced
- 2 cups fresh spinach leaves
- 1/4 cup cherry tomatoes, halved
- 1/4 cup cucumber, sliced
- 2 tablespoons red onion, finely chopped
- 2 tablespoons Kalamata olives, pitted and sliced
- 2 tablespoons feta cheese, crumbled
- 2 tablespoons Greek yogurt
- 1 tablespoon extra-virgin olive oil
- 1 tablespoon lemon juice
- 1/2 teaspoon dried oregano
- Salt and black pepper to taste

Directions

1. In a large bowl, combine grilled chicken slices, fresh spinach, cherry tomatoes, cucumber, red onion, Kalamata olives, and feta cheese.
2. In a separate bowl, whisk together Greek yogurt, olive oil, lemon juice, dried oregano, salt, and pepper to make the dressing.
3. Drizzle the dressing over the salad and toss.
4. Enjoy your Greek-style chicken and spinach salad, a taste of Rhodes.

Chapter 3:
Dinner Delights, Few Carbs

1 fillet   350   10

Baked Salmon with Lemon and Dill

Enjoy a light and flavorful dinner with baked salmon, kissed by the brightness of lemon and the freshness of dill.
A dish inspired by coastal Scandinavia, where salmon is a prized catch.

Ingredients:

- 1 salmon fillet (6 oz)
- 1 lemon, thinly sliced
- 1 tablespoon fresh dill, chopped
- 1 tablespoon olive oil
- Salt and black pepper to taste

Directions

1. Preheat your oven to 375°F (190°C).
2. Place salmon fillet on a baking sheet.
3. Season with salt and pepper.
4. Top with lemon slices and dill. Drizzle with olive oil.
5. Bake for 15-20 minutes until salmon flakes easily with a fork.
6. Serve and savor the Scandinavian flavors of baked salmon.

1 fillet — 300 — 15

Greek-Style Grilled Swordfish

Dive into the Mediterranean sea with Greek-style grilled swordfish, marinated in herbs and spices.
A dish reminiscent of the Aegean shores, where fish is celebrated.

Ingredients:

- 1 swordfish fillet (6 oz)
- 1/4 cup Greek yogurt
- 1 tablespoon fresh oregano, chopped
- 1 clove garlic, minced
- 1 tablespoon lemon juice
- 1 tablespoon olive oil
- Salt and black pepper to taste

Directions

1. In a bowl, combine Greek yogurt, oregano, garlic, lemon juice, olive oil, salt, and pepper.
2. Marinate swordfish in the mixture for 10 minutes.
3. Preheat grill to medium-high heat.
4. Grill swordfish for 3-4 minutes per side until it flakes easily.
5. Serve your Greek-style grilled swordfish with a taste of the Aegean.

1 serving   280   20

Garlic Shrimp with Roasted Asparagus

Delight in the succulence of garlic shrimp paired with roasted asparagus.
A dish that mirrors the flavors of the Mediterranean coastline.

Ingredients:

- 8 large shrimp, peeled and deveined
- 1 bunch asparagus, trimmed
- 3 cloves garlic, minced
- 2 tablespoons olive oil
- 1 tablespoon fresh parsley, chopped
- Lemon wedges for garnish
- Salt and black pepper to taste

Directions

1. Preheat your oven to 400°F (200°C).
2. Toss shrimp and asparagus with minced garlic, olive oil, salt, and pepper.
3. Place on a baking sheet.
4. Roast for 10-12 minutes until shrimp are pink and asparagus is tender.
5. Garnish with fresh parsley and lemon wedges.
6. Serve your Mediterranean-inspired garlic shrimp and asparagus.

1 serving   380   30

Mediterranean Chicken Thighs with Olives

Indulge in tender Mediterranean chicken thighs, simmered with olives and aromatic herbs. A dish that brings the warmth of Greece to your dinner table.

Ingredients:

- 2 chicken thighs
- 1/4 cup Kalamata olives, pitted
- 1/4 cup cherry tomatoes, halved
- 2 cloves garlic, minced
- 1/2 teaspoon dried oregano
- 1/2 teaspoon dried thyme
- 1/4 cup chicken broth
- 1 tablespoon fresh parsley, chopped
- Salt and black pepper to taste

Directions

1. Season chicken thighs with oregano, thyme, salt, and pepper.
2. Heat olive oil in a skillet over medium-high heat.
3. Brown chicken thighs on both sides.
4. Add garlic, olives, and cherry tomatoes. Sauté briefly.
5. Pour in chicken broth.
6. Cover and simmer for 20-25 minutes until chicken is cooked through.
7. Garnish with fresh parsley.
8. Savor the flavors of Greece with your Mediterranean chicken thighs.

1 serving   320   45

Keto Eggplant Parmesan

Delight in a low-carb twist on the Italian classic
- Keto Eggplant Parmesan.
A dish that brings the heart of Italy to your
dinner plate.

Ingredients:

- 1 medium eggplant, sliced into rounds
- 1/2 cup almond flour
- 1/4 cup grated Parmesan cheese
- 1/2 teaspoon dried basil
- 1/2 teaspoon dried oregano
- 1 cup tomato sauce
- 1 1/2 cups shredded mozzarella cheese
- Fresh basil leaves for garnish
- Salt and black pepper to taste

Directions

1. Preheat your oven to 375°F (190°C).
2. In one bowl, combine almond flour, grated Parmesan, dried basil, dried oregano, salt, and pepper.
3. Dip eggplant slices into the mixture to coat.
4. Place on a baking sheet and bake for 20 minutes until tender.
5. In a baking dish, layer tomato sauce, eggplant slices, and mozzarella cheese. Repeat.
6. Bake for 20 minutes until bubbly and golden.
7. Garnish with fresh basil.
8. Enjoy your keto Eggplant Parmesan, a taste of Italy with fewer carbs.

1 serving   280   25

Immerse yourself in the bright flavors of lemon and herbs with baked cod served alongside roasted vegetables.
A dish inspired by the coastal regions of France, where simplicity meets sophistication.

Lemon Herb Baked Cod with Vegetables

Ingredients:

- 1 cod fillet (6 oz)
- 1/2 lemon, thinly sliced
- 1 tablespoon fresh parsley, chopped
- 1 clove garlic, minced
- 1 cup mixed vegetables (zucchini, bell peppers, cherry tomatoes)
- 1 tablespoon olive oil
- Salt and black pepper to taste

Directions

1. Preheat your oven to 375°F (190°C).
2. Season cod fillet with minced garlic, fresh parsley, lemon slices, salt, and pepper.
3. Place cod on a baking sheet.
4. Toss mixed vegetables with olive oil, salt, and pepper.
5. Arrange vegetables around the cod.
6. Bake for 20-25 minutes until cod flakes easily and vegetables are tender.
7. Serve your lemon herb baked cod with a taste of coastal France.

1 serving 400 30

Mediterranean Lamb Chops with Tzatziki

Indulge in the rich flavors of Mediterranean lamb chops served with creamy tzatziki sauce. A dish that captures the essence of Greek feasting.

Ingredients:

- 2 lamb chops
- 1/4 cup Greek yogurt
- 1/2 cucumber, grated
- 1 clove garlic, minced
- 1 tablespoon fresh dill, chopped
- 1 tablespoon fresh mint, chopped
- 1 tablespoon lemon juice
- 1 tablespoon olive oil
- Salt and black pepper to taste

Directions

1. Season lamb chops with salt, pepper, and olive oil.
2. Heat a grill or skillet to medium-high heat. Grill lamb chops for 3-4 minutes per side for medium-rare.
3. In a bowl, combine Greek yogurt, grated cucumber, minced garlic, dill, mint, lemon juice, salt, and pepper to make tzatziki sauce.
4. Serve lamb chops with tzatziki on the side.
5. Savor the flavors of Greece with your Mediterranean lamb chops.

1
mushroom

240

35

Italian Stuffed Portobello Mushrooms

Delight in Italian flavors with stuffed Portobello mushrooms, brimming with herbs and cheese. A dish that pays tribute to the rustic kitchens of Tuscany.

Ingredients:

- 1 large Portobello mushroom cap
- 1/4 cup ricotta cheese
- 1/4 cup spinach, chopped
- 1/4 cup cherry tomatoes, diced
- 1/4 cup grated Parmesan cheese
- 1 clove garlic, minced
- 1/2 teaspoon dried basil
- 1/2 teaspoon dried oregano
- 1 tablespoon olive oil
- Salt and black pepper to taste

Directions

1. Preheat your oven to 375°F (190°C).
2. Remove the stem and gills from the mushroom cap.
3. In a bowl, combine ricotta cheese, chopped spinach, diced tomatoes, grated Parmesan, minced garlic, dried basil, dried oregano, salt, and pepper.
4. Stuff the mushroom cap with this mixture.
5. Drizzle olive oil on top.
6. Bake for 25-30 minutes until the mushroom is tender and the stuffing is golden.
7. Enjoy your Italian stuffed Portobello mushroom, a taste of Tuscany on your plate.

Substitutions

-

1 serving 320 20

Low-Carb Mediterranean Beef Stir-Fry

Savor the flavors of the Mediterranean with a low-carb beef stir-fry, packed with colorful vegetables and aromatic spices.
A dish that celebrates the culinary diversity of the Mediterranean.

Ingredients:

- 4 oz lean beef strips
- 1/2 cup bell peppers, sliced
- 1/2 cup zucchini, sliced
- 1/4 cup red onion, thinly sliced
- 1/4 cup cherry tomatoes, halved
- 1 clove garlic, minced
- 1/2 teaspoon dried oregano
- 1/2 teaspoon dried thyme
- 1 tablespoon olive oil
- Salt and black pepper to taste

Directions

1. Heat olive oil in a skillet over high heat.
2. Add beef strips and cook until browned. Remove from the skillet.
3. In the same skillet, sauté garlic, bell peppers, zucchini, and red onion until tender.
4. Return beef to the skillet.
5. Add cherry tomatoes, oregano, thyme, salt, and pepper.
6. Stir-fry for another 2-3 minutes.
7. Serve your low-carb Mediterranean beef stir-fry and enjoy the diverse flavors.

1 serving 160 15

Lemon and Garlic Grilled Zucchini

Elevate the simplicity of zucchini with the zing of lemon and the warmth of garlic.
A dish that mirrors the passion for fresh ingredients in Italian cuisine.

Ingredients:

- 1 zucchini, sliced
- 1 tablespoon olive oil
- 1 clove garlic, minced
- Zest and juice of 1 lemon
- 1/2 teaspoon dried basil
- 1/2 teaspoon dried oregano
- Salt and black pepper to taste

Directions

1. Preheat your grill or grill pan to medium-high heat.
2. In a bowl, combine sliced zucchini, olive oil, minced garlic, lemon zest, lemon juice, dried basil, dried oregano, salt, and pepper.
3. Toss to coat.
4. Grill zucchini for 3-4 minutes per side until tender and slightly charred.
5. Serve your lemon and garlic grilled zucchini with the zest of Italian flavors.

Chapter 4:
Low-Carb Mediterranean Vegetable Sides

1 serving | 120 | 20

Greek-Style Roasted Cauliflower

Elevate cauliflower with Mediterranean flair in this Greek-style roasted dish.
A side inspired by the rustic kitchens of Crete.

Ingredients:

- 1 small cauliflower head, cut into florets
- 2 tablespoons olive oil
- 1 teaspoon dried oregano
- 1 teaspoon dried thyme
- 2 cloves garlic, minced
- 1/4 cup Kalamata olives, pitted and sliced
- 2 tablespoons fresh parsley, chopped
- Salt and black pepper to taste

Directions

1. Preheat your oven to 425°F (220°C).
2. In a large bowl, toss cauliflower florets with olive oil, dried oregano, dried thyme, minced garlic, salt, and pepper.
3. Spread cauliflower on a baking sheet.
4. Roast for 20-25 minutes until tender and golden.
5. Remove from the oven and sprinkle Kalamata olives and fresh parsley on top.
6. Enjoy your Greek-style roasted cauliflower, a taste of Crete.

1 serving 160 15

Mediterranean Grilled Eggplant

Enjoy the simplicity of Mediterranean grilled eggplant, seasoned to perfection.
A side that captures the essence of coastal Turkey.

Ingredients:

- 1 small eggplant, sliced
- 2 tablespoons olive oil
- 1 teaspoon dried basil
- 1 teaspoon dried oregano
- 1 clove garlic, minced
- 1 tablespoon lemon juice
- Salt and black pepper to taste

Directions

1. Preheat your grill or grill pan to medium-high heat.
2. In a bowl, combine eggplant slices, olive oil, dried basil, dried oregano, minced garlic, lemon juice, salt, and pepper.
3. Toss to coat.
4. Grill eggplant slices for 3-4 minutes per side until tender and slightly charred.
5. Remove from the grill and serve.
6. Enjoy your Mediterranean grilled eggplant, a taste of coastal Turkey.

1 serving 100 20

Lemon and Garlic Roasted Brussels Sprouts

Roasted Brussels sprouts with the zing of lemon and the warmth of garlic.
A side inspired by the family gatherings of Sicily.

Ingredients:

- 1 cup Brussels sprouts, trimmed and halved
- 1 tablespoon olive oil
- Zest and juice of 1 lemon
- 2 cloves garlic, minced
- 1 teaspoon dried thyme
- Salt and black pepper to taste

Directions

1. Preheat your oven to 400°F (200°C).
2. In a bowl, toss Brussels sprouts with olive oil, lemon zest, lemon juice, minced garlic, dried thyme, salt, and pepper.
3. Spread Brussels sprouts on a baking sheet.
4. Roast for 20-25 minutes until tender and crispy.
5. Remove from the oven and serve.
6. Enjoy your lemon and garlic roasted Brussels sprouts, a taste of Sicily.

1 serving   180   25

Greek Zucchini Fritters

Crispy and flavorful Greek zucchini fritters, a delightful side dish.
A side that celebrates the local markets of Athens.

Ingredients:

- 1 medium zucchini, grated and drained
- 1/4 cup crumbled feta cheese
- 1/4 cup fresh dill, chopped
- 1/4 cup fresh parsley, chopped
- 2 cloves garlic, minced
- 1/4 cup almond flour
- 1 egg
- Salt and black pepper to taste

Directions

1. In a bowl, combine grated zucchini, crumbled feta cheese, fresh dill, fresh parsley, minced garlic, almond flour, egg, salt, and pepper.
2. Mix until well combined.
3. Heat olive oil in a skillet over medium-high heat.
4. Drop spoonfuls of the zucchini mixture into the hot skillet and flatten to form fritters.
5. Cook for 3-4 minutes per side until golden and crispy.
6. Remove from the skillet and drain on paper towels.
7. Serve your Greek zucchini fritters, a taste of Athens.

1 serving | 140 | 20

Mediterranean Broccoli Salad

Delight in a refreshing Mediterranean broccoli salad, bursting with flavors.
A side inspired by the garden feasts of Provence.

Ingredients:

- 1 cup broccoli florets, blanched and chopped
- 1/4 cup cherry tomatoes, halved
- 1/4 cup red bell pepper, diced
- 1/4 cup cucumber, diced
- 2 tablespoons red onion, finely chopped
- 2 tablespoons feta cheese, crumbled
- 2 tablespoons fresh parsley, chopped
- 2 tablespoons extra-virgin olive oil
- 1 tablespoon lemon juice
- Salt and black pepper to taste

Directions

1. In a bowl, combine blanched and chopped broccoli florets, cherry tomatoes, red bell pepper, cucumber, red onion, feta cheese, and fresh parsley.
2. In a separate bowl, whisk together olive oil, lemon juice, salt, and pepper to make the dressing.
3. Drizzle the dressing over the salad and toss.
4. Enjoy your Mediterranean broccoli salad, a taste of Provence.

1 serving | 120 | 20

Italian Baked Parmesan Tomatoes

Baked Parmesan tomatoes with Italian flair, a delightful side dish.
A side inspired by the cozy kitchens of Tuscany.

Ingredients:

- 2 ripe tomatoes, sliced
- 2 tablespoons grated Parmesan cheese
- 1 clove garlic, minced
- 1 teaspoon dried basil
- 1 teaspoon dried oregano
- 2 tablespoons extra-virgin olive oil
- Salt and black pepper to taste

Directions

1. Preheat your oven to 375°F (190°C).
2. Place tomato slices on a baking sheet.
3. In a bowl, combine grated Parmesan cheese, minced garlic, dried basil, dried oregano, olive oil, salt, and pepper.
4. Spoon the Parmesan mixture onto each tomato slice.
5. Bake for 15-20 minutes until tomatoes are tender and the topping is golden.
6. Serve your Italian baked Parmesan tomatoes, a taste of Tuscany.

1 serving   90   20

Roasted Asparagus with Feta and Lemon

Roasted asparagus enhanced with the tang of feta and the brightness of lemon.
A side inspired by the Mediterranean gardens of Santorini.

Ingredients:

- 1 bunch asparagus spears, trimmed
- 2 tablespoons crumbled feta cheese
- Zest and juice of 1 lemon
- 2 tablespoons extra-virgin olive oil
- Salt and black pepper to taste

Directions

1. Preheat your oven to 425°F (220°C).
2. Place trimmed asparagus spears on a baking sheet.
3. Drizzle with olive oil, lemon zest, lemon juice, salt, and pepper. Toss to coat.
4. Roast for 12-15 minutes until asparagus is tender and slightly crispy.
5. Remove from the oven and sprinkle crumbled feta on top.
6. Serve your roasted asparagus with feta and lemon, a taste of Santorini.

1 serving   80   10

Low-Carb Mediterranean Cucumber Salad

Enjoy a light and refreshing low-carb Mediterranean cucumber salad.
A side that echoes the breezy coasts of Cyprus.

Ingredients:

- 1 cucumber, sliced
- 1/4 cup cherry tomatoes, halved
- 2 tablespoons red onion, finely chopped
- 2 tablespoons fresh mint, chopped
- 2 tablespoons extra-virgin olive oil
- 1 tablespoon red wine vinegar
- Salt and black pepper to taste

Directions

1. In a bowl, combine sliced cucumber, cherry tomatoes, red onion, and fresh mint.
2. In a separate bowl, whisk together olive oil, red wine vinegar, salt, and pepper to make the dressing.
3. Drizzle the dressing over the salad and toss.
4. Enjoy your low-carb Mediterranean cucumber salad, a taste of Cyprus.

1 serving   160   30

Lemon and Herb Roasted Artichokes

Indulge in lemon and herb roasted artichokes, a Mediterranean side dish.
A side inspired by the traditional kitchens of Greece.

Ingredients:

- 2 whole artichokes, trimmed and halved
- 2 tablespoons olive oil
- Zest and juice of 1 lemon
- 2 cloves garlic, minced
- 2 tablespoons fresh parsley, chopped
- 1 tablespoon fresh dill, chopped
- Salt and black pepper to taste

Directions

1. Preheat your oven to 375°F (190°C).
2. Place trimmed and halved artichokes in a baking dish.
3. Drizzle with olive oil, lemon zest, lemon juice, minced garlic, salt, and pepper. Toss to coat.
4. Sprinkle chopped fresh parsley and fresh dill on top.
5. Cover the baking dish with aluminum foil.
6. Roast for 25-30 minutes.
7. Remove the foil and roast for an additional 15-20 minutes until artichokes are tender and slightly crispy.
8. Serve your lemon and herb roasted artichokes, a taste of Greece.

1 serving | 180 | 40

Mediterranean Spaghetti Squash

Enjoy the Mediterranean twist on spaghetti squash, a low-carb side dish.
A side inspired by the sunny gardens of Provence.

Ingredients:

- 1 small spaghetti squash, halved and seeded
- 2 tablespoons extra-virgin olive oil
- 1 clove garlic, minced
- 1/4 cup cherry tomatoes, halved
- 1/4 cup Kalamata olives, pitted and sliced
- 2 tablespoons fresh basil, chopped
- 2 tablespoons fresh parsley, chopped
- Salt and black pepper to taste

Directions

1. Preheat your oven to 375°F (190°C).
2. Place spaghetti squash halves, cut side down, on a baking sheet.
3. Roast for 30-35 minutes until the squash is tender and can be easily shredded with a fork.
4. While the squash is roasting, heat olive oil in a skillet over medium heat.
5. Add minced garlic and sauté for 1-2 minutes until fragrant.
6. Add cherry tomatoes, Kalamata olives, fresh basil, fresh parsley, salt, and pepper. Sauté for 3-4 minutes until tomatoes are softened.
7. Use a fork to shred the cooked spaghetti squash into strands.
8. Toss the squash with the Mediterranean tomato and olive mixture.
9. Serve your Mediterranean spaghetti squash, a taste of Provence.

We have a small favor to ask

Reviews are a lifeline for authors and small publishers like us. They provide valuable feedback and help us reach more readers. If you've been enjoying our book so far, we kindly ask for a moment of your time.

Please consider going back to your app or the platform where you made your purchase. Look for the review button and share your thoughts with us. A simple rating and a short sentence would mean the world to us.

Being a small publisher, reviews are hard to come by, and your review could make a significant difference in helping us grow. We genuinely appreciate every word you share, and we read every single review with gratitude.

Now, let's return to the delicious recipes that brought us together in the first place.

Thank you for your support!

Chapter 5:
Sweet and Low-Carb Mediterranean Endings

1 serving · 180 · 10

Greek Yogurt with Berries and Nuts

Satisfy your sweet tooth with a bowl of Greek yogurt topped with luscious berries and crunchy nuts.
A dessert that brings the flavors of the Greek islands to your table.

Ingredients:

- 1/2 cup Greek yogurt
- 1/4 cup mixed berries (strawberries, blueberries, raspberries)
- 2 tablespoons mixed nuts (almonds, walnuts, pistachios), chopped
- 1 tablespoon honey (optional)

Directions

1. In a bowl, spoon Greek yogurt.
2. Top with mixed berries and chopped nuts.
3. Drizzle honey over the yogurt if desired.
4. Serve your Greek yogurt with berries and nuts, a taste of the Greek islands.

2 strawberries 60 15

Dark Chocolate-Dipped Strawberries

Indulge in the simple pleasure of dark chocolate-dipped strawberries.
A sweet treat reminiscent of romantic evenings on the Amalfi Coast.

Ingredients:

- 4 fresh strawberries, washed and dried
- 1 oz dark chocolate (70% cocoa or higher), chopped
- 1/2 teaspoon coconut oil (optional)

Directions

1. In a microwave-safe bowl, melt dark chocolate and coconut oil (if using) in 15-second intervals, stirring in between until smooth.
2. Dip each strawberry into the melted chocolate, allowing any excess to drip off.
3. Place the dipped strawberries on a parchment paper-lined tray.
4. Chill in the refrigerator for 10-15 minutes until the chocolate hardens.
5. Serve your dark chocolate-dipped strawberries, a taste of the Amalfi Coast.

1 slice   220   40

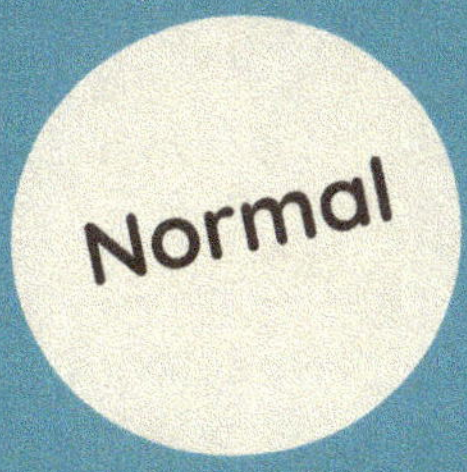

Almond and Orange Blossom Ricotta Tart

Delight in a slice of almond and orange blossom ricotta tart, a Mediterranean dessert masterpiece.
A tart that reflects the charm of Sicilian patisseries.

Ingredients:

- 1 pre-made almond flour pie crust
- 1 cup ricotta cheese
- 1/4 cup almond meal
- 1/4 cup powdered erythritol or your preferred low-carb sweetener
- Zest of 1 orange
- 2 tablespoons fresh orange juice
- 1/2 teaspoon orange blossom water (optional)
- 1/4 teaspoon almond extract
- 1 egg
- 2 tablespoons sliced almonds

Directions

1. Preheat your oven to 350°F (175°C).
2. In a bowl, combine ricotta cheese, almond meal, powdered erythritol, orange zest, fresh orange juice, orange blossom water (if using), and almond extract. Mix well.
3. Add the egg and mix until the filling is smooth.
4. Pour the ricotta mixture into the almond flour pie crust.
5. Sprinkle sliced almonds on top.
6. Bake for 25-30 minutes until the tart is set and lightly golden.
7. Remove from the oven and let it cool.
8. Slice and serve your almond and orange blossom ricotta tart, a taste of Sicily.

2
cookies

90

20

Low-Carb Mediterranean Almond Cookies

Enjoy guilt-free indulgence with low-carb Mediterranean almond cookies.
Cookies that pay tribute to the bakeries of Athens.

Ingredients:

- 1 cup almond flour
- 2 tablespoons powdered erythritol or your preferred low-carb sweetener
- 1/4 teaspoon baking powder
- 1/4 cup unsalted butter, softened
- 1/2 teaspoon almond extract
- 1 egg
- 1/4 cup sliced almonds

Directions

1. Preheat your oven to 350°F (175°C).
2. In a bowl, combine almond flour, powdered erythritol, and baking powder. Mix well.
3. In another bowl, cream together softened butter and almond extract.
4. Add the egg to the butter mixture and beat until smooth.
5. Gradually add the dry ingredients to the wet ingredients and mix until a dough forms.
6. Roll the dough into 12 small balls and place them on a parchment paper-lined baking sheet.
7. Flatten each ball with a fork and press sliced almonds onto the tops of the cookies.
8. Bake for 10-12 minutes until the cookies are lightly golden.
9. Remove from the oven and let them cool.
10. Enjoy your low-carb Mediterranean almond cookies, a taste of Athens.

1 serving   80   20

Lemon Sorbet with Fresh Mint

Refresh your palate with lemon sorbet garnished with fresh mint leaves.
A sorbet that evokes the breezy streets of Mykonos.

Ingredients:

- 1 cup water
- 1/2 cup lemon juice (from fresh lemons)
- 1/2 cup powdered erythritol or your preferred low-carb sweetener
- Zest of 1 lemon
- 2 tablespoons fresh mint leaves, chopped

Directions

1. In a saucepan, combine water, lemon juice, powdered erythritol, and lemon zest. Heat over medium heat, stirring until the sweetener is dissolved.
2. Remove from heat and let the mixture cool.
3. Pour the lemon mixture into an ice cream maker and churn according to the manufacturer's instructions.
4. Once the sorbet reaches a soft-serve consistency, transfer it to a lidded container and freeze for at least 2 hours or until firm.
5. Serve your lemon sorbet garnished with fresh mint leaves, a taste of Mykonos.

1 serving   150   30

Mediterranean Chia Seed Pudding

Dive into the creaminess of Mediterranean chia seed pudding, a guilt-free dessert.
A pudding inspired by the kitchens of Barcelona.

Ingredients:

- 2 tablespoons chia seeds
- 1/2 cup unsweetened almond milk
- 1/4 cup Greek yogurt
- 1/4 cup mixed berries (strawberries, blueberries, raspberries)
- 1 tablespoon powdered erythritol or your preferred low-carb sweetener
- 1/2 teaspoon vanilla extract
- 1/4 teaspoon ground cinnamon

Directions

1. In a bowl, combine chia seeds, almond milk, Greek yogurt, powdered erythritol, vanilla extract, and ground cinnamon. Mix well.
2. Cover and refrigerate the mixture for at least 30 minutes or overnight to allow it to thicken.
3. Before serving, top the chia seed pudding with mixed berries.
4. Enjoy your Mediterranean chia seed pudding, a taste of Barcelona.

2 bites | 160 | 30

Greek Yogurt Cheesecake Bites

Savor the creamy delight of Greek yogurt cheesecake bites.
Bites that transport you to the hills of Crete.

Ingredients:

- 1/2 cup almond flour
- 2 tablespoons powdered erythritol or your preferred low-carb sweetener
- 2 tablespoons unsalted butter, melted
- 1/2 cup cream cheese, softened
- 1/4 cup Greek yogurt
- 1 egg
- 1/2 teaspoon vanilla extract
- Zest of 1 lemon
- 1/4 cup mixed berries (strawberries, blueberries, raspberries) for garnish (optional)

Directions

1. Preheat your oven to 325°F (160°C).
2. In a bowl, combine almond flour, powdered erythritol, and melted butter. Mix until it forms a crumbly texture.
3. Line a mini muffin tin with paper liners. Press a spoonful of the almond flour mixture into each liner as the crust.
4. In another bowl, beat together cream cheese, Greek yogurt, egg, vanilla extract, and lemon zest until smooth.
5. Spoon the cream cheese mixture over the almond flour crust in each liner.
6. Bake for 18-20 minutes until the cheesecake bites are set and slightly golden around the edges.
7. Allow them to cool and refrigerate for at least 2 hours or until firm.
8. Garnish with mixed berries if desired.
9. Enjoy your Greek yogurt cheesecake bites, a taste of Crete.

1 piece   180   40

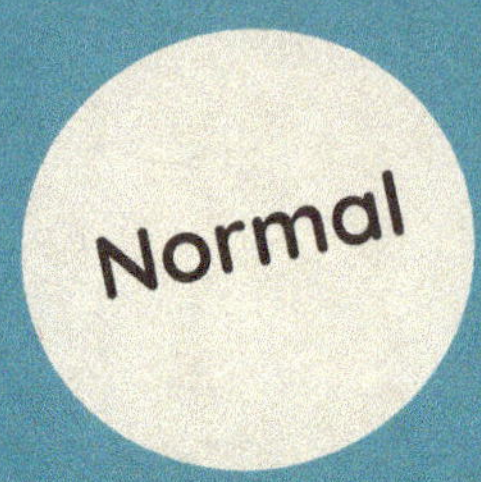

Keto Baklava with Almonds and Walnuts

Delight in the layers of keto baklava, a nutty and sweet Mediterranean treat.
A dessert inspired by the bakeries of Istanbul.

Ingredients:

- 1 cup almond flour
- 1/4 cup powdered erythritol or your preferred low-carb sweetener
- 1/4 cup unsalted butter, melted
- 1/2 cup mixed nuts (almonds, walnuts), finely chopped
- 1 teaspoon ground cinnamon
- 1/4 teaspoon ground cloves
- 1/4 teaspoon ground cardamom
- Zest of 1 lemon
- 1/4 cup sugar-free honey or a sugar-free syrup of your choice (for the syrup)
- 1/4 cup water (for the syrup)
- 1/2 teaspoon lemon juice (for the syrup)
- 1/4 teaspoon vanilla extract (for the syrup)

Directions

1. Preheat your oven to 325°F (160°C).
2. In a bowl, combine almond flour, powdered erythritol, melted butter, finely chopped mixed nuts, ground cinnamon, ground cloves, ground cardamom, and lemon zest. Mix until it forms a sticky dough.
3. Press half of the dough into the bottom of a greased 8x8-inch baking dish to form the bottom layer.
4. Bake the bottom layer for 12-15 minutes until it's slightly golden.
5. While the bottom layer is baking, make the syrup. In a small saucepan, combine sugar-free honey or syrup, water, lemon juice, and vanilla extract. Bring to a simmer and cook for 5 minutes.
6. Remove the bottom layer from the oven and pour half of the syrup over it.
7. Sprinkle the remaining dough over the syrup to create the top layer.
8. Bake for an additional 20-25 minutes until the top layer is golden.
9. Remove from the oven and pour the remaining syrup over the top layer while it's still hot.
10. Allow it to cool and set before cutting into pieces.
11. Enjoy your keto baklava with almonds and walnuts, a taste of Istanbul.

1 serving   120   15

Low-Carb Mediterranean Berry Parfait

Savor a low-carb Mediterranean berry parfait, a delightful blend of flavors and textures. A dessert that captures the essence of the French Riviera.

Ingredients:

- 1/4 cup Greek yogurt
- 1/4 cup mixed berries (strawberries, blueberries, raspberries)
- 1 tablespoon chopped nuts (almonds, walnuts, pistachios)
- 1/2 teaspoon honey (optional)

Directions

1. In a glass or serving dish, spoon a layer of Greek yogurt.
2. Add a layer of mixed berries on top of the yogurt.
3. Sprinkle chopped nuts over the berries.
4. Drizzle honey over the parfait if desired.
5. Repeat the layers until you've used all the ingredients.
6. Enjoy your low-carb Mediterranean berry parfait, a taste of the French Riviera.

1 slice

180

40

Almond and Orange Blossom Semolina Cake (Low-Carb)

Delight in a slice of almond and orange blossom semolina cake with a Mediterranean twist.
A cake that transports you to the sunny groves of Valencia.

Ingredients:

- 1/2 cup almond flour
- 1/4 cup semolina flour (or almond flour for a gluten-free option)
- 1/4 cup powdered erythritol or your preferred low-carb sweetener
- 1/4 cup unsalted butter, melted
- 1/4 cup plain Greek yogurt
- 1 egg
- Zest of 1 orange
- 1/2 teaspoon orange blossom water (optional)
- 1/4 teaspoon almond extract
- 1/2 teaspoon baking powder
- 1/4 teaspoon salt
- 1/4 cup sliced almonds

Directions

1. Preheat your oven to 350°F (175°C).
2. Grease a small baking dish or loaf pan.
3. In a bowl, combine almond flour, semolina flour, powdered erythritol, melted butter, Greek yogurt, egg, orange zest, orange blossom water (if using), almond extract, baking powder, and salt. Mix until well combined.
4. Pour the batter into the greased baking dish.
5. Sprinkle sliced almonds on top.
6. Bake for 25-30 minutes until the cake is set and lightly golden.
7. Remove from the oven and let it cool.
8. Slice and serve your almond and orange blossom semolina cake, a taste of Valencia.

Chapter 6:
Low-Carb Mediterranean Seafood Delights

1 serving   250   20

Mediterranean Shrimp Scampi

Dive into a plate of Mediterranean shrimp scampi, a garlicky and buttery delight.
A dish inspired by the coastal kitchens of Naples.

Ingredients:

- 8 large shrimp, peeled and deveining
- 2 tablespoons unsalted butter
- 2 cloves garlic, minced
- Zest and juice of 1 lemon
- 2 tablespoons fresh parsley, chopped
- 1/4 cup white wine (optional)
- Salt and black pepper to taste

Directions

1. In a skillet, melt the butter over medium-high heat.
2. Add minced garlic and sauté for 1-2 minutes until fragrant.
3. Add the shrimp and cook for 2-3 minutes per side until they turn pink and opaque.
4. If using, pour in white wine and simmer for 2 minutes to reduce.
5. Stir in lemon zest, lemon juice, chopped fresh parsley, salt, and black pepper.
6. Serve your Mediterranean shrimp scampi, a taste of Naples.

1 serving | 180 | 30

Enjoy the tender and flavorful grilled octopus with a zesty lemon and herb marinade.
A dish that echoes the coastal tavernas of Santorini.

Grilled Octopus with Lemon and Herbs

Ingredients:

- 1 octopus tentacle, cleaned and tenderized
- 2 tablespoons extra-virgin olive oil
- Zest and juice of 1 lemon
- 2 cloves garlic, minced
- 1 tablespoon fresh oregano, chopped
- 1 tablespoon fresh parsley, chopped
- Salt and black pepper to taste

Directions

1. Preheat your grill to medium-high heat.
2. In a bowl, whisk together olive oil, lemon zest, lemon juice, minced garlic, fresh oregano, fresh parsley, salt, and black pepper to make the marinade.
3. Brush the octopus tentacle with the marinade.
4. Grill the octopus for 2-3 minutes per side until charred and tender.
5. Remove from the grill and let it rest for a few minutes.
6. Slice and serve your grilled octopus with lemon and herbs, a taste of Santorini.

1 serving   280   30

Baked Trout with Mediterranean Salsa

Indulge in baked trout topped with a vibrant Mediterranean salsa.
A dish inspired by the fishermen's feasts of Corsica.

Ingredients:

- 1 trout fillet (6-8 oz)
- 1 tablespoon extra-virgin olive oil
- 1/2 teaspoon dried oregano
- 1/2 teaspoon dried thyme
- 1 clove garlic, minced
- 1/4 cup cherry tomatoes, halved
- 2 tablespoons Kalamata olives, pitted and sliced
- 1 tablespoon red onion, finely chopped
- 1 tablespoon fresh parsley, chopped
- Zest and juice of 1 lemon
- Salt and black pepper to taste

Directions

1. Preheat your oven to 375°F (190°C).
2. Place the trout fillet on a baking sheet lined with parchment paper.
3. Drizzle with olive oil and sprinkle dried oregano, dried thyme, minced garlic, salt, and black pepper.
4. Bake for 15-18 minutes until the trout flakes easily with a fork.
5. While the trout is baking, make the Mediterranean salsa. In a bowl, combine halved cherry tomatoes, sliced Kalamata olives, finely chopped red onion, chopped fresh parsley, lemon zest, and lemon juice. Mix well.
6. Serve the baked trout with a generous spoonful of Mediterranean salsa, a taste of Corsica.

1 serving   200   15

Lemon and Herb Seared Scallops

Delight in seared scallops with a zesty lemon and herb drizzle.
A dish inspired by the seaside bistros of Nice.

Ingredients:

- 4 large scallops
- 1 tablespoon extra-virgin olive oil
- 2 cloves garlic, minced
- Zest and juice of 1 lemon
- 1 tablespoon fresh parsley, chopped
- 1 tablespoon fresh chives, chopped
- Salt and black pepper to taste

Directions

1. Heat olive oil in a skillet over medium-high heat.
2. Season scallops with salt and black pepper.
3. Sear scallops for 2-3 minutes per side until they develop a golden crust and are opaque in the center.
4. Remove scallops from the skillet and set aside.
5. In the same skillet, add minced garlic and sauté for 1-2 minutes until fragrant.
6. Stir in lemon zest, lemon juice, chopped fresh parsley, and chopped fresh chives.
7. Pour the lemon and herb drizzle over the seared scallops.
8. Serve your lemon and herb seared scallops, a taste of Nice.

1 serving   280   20

Keto Mediterranean Tuna Steak

Enjoy a keto Mediterranean tuna steak, grilled to perfection with Mediterranean flavors.
A dish reminiscent of the coastal villages of Crete.

Ingredients:

- 1 tuna steak (6-8 oz)
- 2 tablespoons extra-virgin olive oil
- 2 cloves garlic, minced
- 1 teaspoon dried oregano
- 1/2 teaspoon smoked paprika
- Zest and juice of 1 lemon
- Salt and black pepper to taste

Directions

1. Preheat your grill to medium-high heat.
2. In a bowl, whisk together olive oil, minced garlic, dried oregano, smoked paprika, lemon zest, lemon juice, salt, and black pepper to make the marinade.
3. Brush the tuna steak with the marinade.
4. Grill the tuna steak for 2-3 minutes per side until it's seared on the outside but still pink in the center.
5. Remove from the grill and let it rest for a few minutes.
6. Serve your keto Mediterranean tuna steak, a taste of Crete.

2 cakes   240   30

Mediterranean Salmon Cakes

Ingredients:

- 1 can (6 oz) pink salmon, drained and flaked
- 1/4 cup almond flour
- 1 egg
- 1/4 cup red bell pepper, finely chopped
- 1/4 cup red onion, finely chopped
- 2 cloves garlic, minced
- 2 tablespoons fresh parsley, chopped
- 1/2 teaspoon dried dill
- 1/4 teaspoon ground cumin
- 1/4 teaspoon smoked paprika
- 2 tablespoons extra-virgin olive oil
- Lemon wedges for serving (optional)
- Salt and black pepper to taste

Savor Mediterranean salmon cakes, a blend of flaky salmon and aromatic herbs.
Cakes that recall the seaside cafes of Barcelona.

Directions

1. In a bowl, combine flaked salmon, almond flour, beaten egg, finely chopped red bell pepper, finely chopped red onion, minced garlic, chopped fresh parsley, dried dill, ground cumin, smoked paprika, salt, and black pepper. Mix until the mixture holds together.
2. Form the mixture into 2 salmon cakes.
3. Heat olive oil in a skillet over medium-high heat.
4. Fry the salmon cakes for 3-4 minutes per side until they are golden and crispy.
5. Serve your Mediterranean salmon cakes with lemon wedges if desired, a taste of Barcelona.

1 serving | 180 | 20

Garlic Butter Lobster Tails

Indulge in garlic butter lobster tails, a luxurious and buttery delight.
A dish that echoes the seafood markets of Venice.

Ingredients:

- 1 lobster tail, shell-on
- 2 tablespoons unsalted butter
- 2 cloves garlic, minced
- 1 tablespoon fresh parsley, chopped
- Lemon wedges for serving (optional)
- Salt and black pepper to taste

Directions

1. Preheat your oven to 425°F (220°C).
2. Using kitchen shears, cut the top shell of the lobster tail lengthwise, exposing the meat.
3. Carefully lift the meat and place it on top of the shell.
4. Season the lobster meat with salt and black pepper.
5. In a small saucepan, melt the unsalted butter over medium heat.
6. Stir in minced garlic and sauté for 1-2 minutes until fragrant.
7. Drizzle the garlic butter over the lobster meat.
8. Place the lobster tail on a baking sheet lined with parchment paper.
9. Bake for 12-15 minutes until the lobster meat is opaque and slightly golden.
10. Garnish with chopped fresh parsley and serve with lemon wedges if desired.
11. Enjoy your garlic butter lobster tails, a taste of Venice.

2
sardines

160

20

Greek-Style Grilled Sardines

Enjoy Greek-style grilled sardines, a simple yet flavorful seafood dish.
A dish inspired by the seaside tavernas of Rhodes.

Ingredients:

- 4 fresh sardines, cleaned and gutted
- 2 tablespoons extra-virgin olive oil
- Juice of 1 lemon
- 2 cloves garlic, minced
- 1 teaspoon dried oregano
- Salt and black pepper to taste

Directions

1. Preheat your grill to medium-high heat.
2. In a bowl, whisk together olive oil, lemon juice, minced garlic, dried oregano, salt, and black pepper to make the marinade.
3. Brush the sardines with the marinade inside and out.
4. Grill the sardines for 3-4 minutes per side until they are charred and cooked through.
5. Serve your Greek-style grilled sardines, a taste of Rhodes.

2
skewers

220

30

Lemon and Herb Swordfish Skewers

Savor lemon and herb swordfish skewers, a delightful seafood treat.
Skewers that evoke the coastal grills of Dubrovnik.

Ingredients:

- 8 swordfish cubes (1-inch each)
- 1 tablespoon extra-virgin olive oil
- Zest and juice of 1 lemon
- 1 clove garlic, minced
- 1 tablespoon fresh rosemary, chopped
- 1 tablespoon fresh thyme, chopped
- Salt and black pepper to taste

Directions

1. Preheat your grill to medium-high heat.
2. In a bowl, whisk together olive oil, lemon zest, lemon juice, minced garlic, chopped fresh rosemary, chopped fresh thyme, salt, and black pepper to make the marinade.
3. Thread the swordfish cubes onto skewers.
4. Brush the swordfish skewers with the marinade.
5. Grill the skewers for 2-3 minutes per side until the swordfish is cooked through and has grill marks.
6. Serve your lemon and herb swordfish skewers, a taste of Dubrovnik.

1 serving | 250 | 40

Low-Carb Mediterranean Seafood Stew

Delight in a low-carb Mediterranean seafood stew, a hearty and flavorful dish.
A stew that recalls the fisherman's wharves of Marseille.

Ingredients:

- 6 large shrimp, peeled and deveined
- 4 mussels, cleaned and debearded
- 4 clams, cleaned
- 4 oz white fish fillet (such as cod or halibut), cut into chunks
- 1/4 cup canned diced tomatoes (no sugar added)
- 1/4 cup chicken broth
- 2 cloves garlic, minced
- 1/4 cup red onion, finely chopped
- 1/4 cup red bell pepper, finely chopped
- 1/4 cup zucchini, finely chopped
- 1/4 cup eggplant, finely chopped
- 1/4 cup fennel bulb, finely chopped
- 1/2 teaspoon dried oregano
- 1/4 teaspoon smoked paprika
- 2 tablespoons fresh parsley, chopped
- 1 tablespoon extra-virgin olive oil
- Salt and black pepper to taste

Directions

1. In a large skillet, heat olive oil over medium-high heat.
2. Add minced garlic, finely chopped red onion, finely chopped red bell pepper, finely chopped zucchini, finely chopped eggplant, finely chopped fennel bulb, dried oregano, smoked paprika, salt, and black pepper. Sauté for 5-7 minutes until the vegetables soften.
3. Add canned diced tomatoes and chicken broth. Bring to a simmer and cook for 5 minutes.
4. Add shrimp, mussels, clams, and chunks of white fish. Cover the skillet and simmer for 7-10 minutes until the seafood is cooked through and the shells of the mussels and clams have opened.
5. Garnish with chopped fresh parsley.
6. Serve your low-carb Mediterranean seafood stew, a taste of Marseille.

Chapter 7:
Lean and Low-Carb Mediterranean Meats

1 serving   280   30

Mediterranean Pork Tenderloin with Olive Tapenade

Indulge in Mediterranean pork tenderloin topped with a flavorful olive tapenade. A dish inspired by the rustic kitchens of Tuscany.

Ingredients:

- 1 pork tenderloin (6-8 oz)
- 1 tablespoon extra-virgin olive oil
- 2 cloves garlic, minced
- 1 teaspoon dried rosemary
- 1/4 teaspoon dried thyme
- Salt and black pepper to taste
- Lemon zest (from 1 lemon) for garnish (optional)

Directions

1. Preheat your oven to 375°F (190°C).
2. Season the pork tenderloin with salt, black pepper, dried rosemary, and dried thyme.
3. Heat olive oil in an oven-safe skillet over medium-high heat.
4. Sear the pork tenderloin on all sides until it develops a golden crust.
5. Transfer the skillet to the preheated oven and roast for 15-18 minutes until the pork reaches an internal temperature of 145°F (63°C).
6. While the pork is roasting, prepare the olive tapenade by mixing together minced garlic and chopped olives.
7. Once the pork is done, let it rest for a few minutes before slicing.
8. Top the pork slices with olive tapenade and garnish with lemon zest if desired.
9. Serve your Mediterranean pork tenderloin, a taste of Tuscany.

2
chicken
thighs

240

30

Italian Balsamic Glazed Chicken Thighs

Enjoy Italian balsamic glazed chicken thighs,
tender and infused with rich flavors.
A dish that evokes the vineyards of Sicily.

Ingredients:

- 2 chicken thighs, bone-in and skin-on
- 2 tablespoons balsamic vinegar
- 1 tablespoon extra-virgin olive oil
- 2 cloves garlic, minced
- 1 teaspoon dried Italian seasoning
- 1/4 teaspoon red pepper flakes (optional)
- Salt and black pepper to taste
- Fresh basil leaves for garnish (optional)

Directions

1. Preheat your oven to 375°F (190°C).
2. Season chicken thighs with salt, black pepper, dried Italian seasoning, and red pepper flakes (if using).
3. Heat olive oil in an oven-safe skillet over medium-high heat.
4. Sear the chicken thighs, skin-side down, until the skin is crispy and golden.
5. Flip the chicken thighs and sear the other side.
6. In a bowl, mix together balsamic vinegar and minced garlic.
7. Drizzle the balsamic mixture over the chicken thighs.
8. Transfer the skillet to the preheated oven and roast for 20-25 minutes until the chicken is cooked through and the glaze is caramelized.
9. Garnish with fresh basil leaves if desired.
10. Serve your Italian balsamic glazed chicken thighs, a taste of Sicily.

2
kebabs

280

25

Keto Greek Lamb Kebabs

Savor keto Greek lamb kebabs, packed with Mediterranean spices and flavors.
Kebabs that transport you to the tavernas of Athens.

Ingredients:

- 1/2 lb ground lamb
- 1/4 cup red onion, finely chopped
- 2 cloves garlic, minced
- 1 tablespoon fresh mint, chopped
- 1 tablespoon fresh parsley, chopped
- 1 teaspoon dried oregano
- 1/2 teaspoon ground cumin
- 1/4 teaspoon smoked paprika
- Salt and black pepper to taste
- Olive oil for brushing

Directions

1. In a bowl, combine ground lamb, finely chopped red onion, minced garlic, chopped fresh mint, chopped fresh parsley, dried oregano, ground cumin, smoked paprika, salt, and black pepper. Mix until well combined.
2. Divide the lamb mixture into two portions and shape them into kebabs around metal skewers or wooden skewers soaked in water.
3. Preheat your grill to medium-high heat.
4. Brush the lamb kebabs with olive oil.
5. Grill the kebabs for 10-12 minutes, turning occasionally, until they are cooked to your desired level of doneness.
6. Serve your keto Greek lamb kebabs, a taste of Athens.

2 kofta | 260 | 25

Low-Carb Mediterranean Beef Kofta

Enjoy low-carb Mediterranean beef kofta, flavorful ground beef skewers with herbs and spices.
Kofta that reminds you of the markets of Istanbul.

Ingredients:

- 1/2 lb ground beef
- 1/4 cup red onion, finely chopped
- 2 cloves garlic, minced
- 1 tablespoon fresh parsley, chopped
- 1 teaspoon ground cumin
- 1/2 teaspoon ground coriander
- 1/4 teaspoon ground paprika
- 1/4 teaspoon ground cinnamon
- Salt and black pepper to taste
- Olive oil for brushing

Directions

1. In a bowl, combine ground beef, finely chopped red onion, minced garlic, chopped fresh parsley, ground cumin, ground coriander, ground paprika, ground cinnamon, salt, and black pepper. Mix until well combined.
2. Divide the beef mixture into two portions and shape them into kofta skewers around metal skewers or wooden skewers soaked in water.
3. Preheat your grill to medium-high heat.
4. Brush the beef kofta with olive oil.
5. Grill the kofta for 10-12 minutes, turning occasionally, until they are cooked to your desired level of doneness.
6. Serve your low-carb Mediterranean beef kofta, a taste of Istanbul.

1 chicken breast

240

25

Garlic and Herb Marinated Chicken Breasts

Delight in garlic and herb marinated chicken breasts, tender and full of Mediterranean flavor.
A dish that transports you to the family tables of Provence.

Ingredients:

- 1 chicken breast (6-8 oz)
- 2 tablespoons extra-virgin olive oil
- 2 cloves garlic, minced
- 1 tablespoon fresh rosemary, chopped
- 1 tablespoon fresh thyme, chopped
- Zest and juice of 1 lemon
- Salt and black pepper to taste

Directions

1. In a bowl, whisk together olive oil, minced garlic, chopped fresh rosemary, chopped fresh thyme, lemon zest, lemon juice, salt, and black pepper to make the marinade.
2. Place the chicken breast in a resealable plastic bag or a shallow dish and pour the marinade over it.
3. Seal the bag or cover the dish and refrigerate for at least 30 minutes, or up to 4 hours, to marinate.
4. Preheat your grill to medium-high heat.
5. Remove the chicken breast from the marinade and discard the marinade.
6. Grill the chicken breast for 6-8 minutes per side until it's cooked through and has grill marks.
7. Let it rest for a few minutes before slicing.
8. Serve your garlic and herb marinated chicken breast, a taste of Provence.

2
mushrooms

180

25

Mediterranean Turkey and Spinach Stuffed Mushrooms

Savor Mediterranean turkey and spinach stuffed mushrooms, a savory and satisfying appetizer.
Stuffed mushrooms that remind you of the cozy cafes of Istanbul.

Ingredients:

- 4 large cremini mushrooms
- 1/4 lb ground turkey
- 1/4 cup fresh spinach, chopped
- 2 cloves garlic, minced
- 2 tablespoons feta cheese, crumbled
- 1 tablespoon fresh parsley, chopped
- 1/4 teaspoon dried oregano
- Salt and black pepper to taste
- Olive oil for brushing

Directions

1. Preheat your oven to 375°F (190°C).
2. Remove the stems from the mushrooms and finely chop them.
3. In a skillet, heat olive oil over medium-high heat.
4. Add minced garlic and chopped mushroom stems. Sauté for 3-4 minutes until they soften.
5. Add ground turkey and cook until it's no longer pink, breaking it into crumbles.
6. Stir in chopped fresh spinach, crumbled feta cheese, chopped fresh parsley, dried oregano, salt, and black pepper. Cook for an additional 2 minutes.
7. Fill each mushroom cap with the turkey and spinach mixture.
8. Place the stuffed mushrooms on a baking sheet lined with parchment paper.
9. Bake for 15-18 minutes until the mushrooms are tender and the filling is golden.
10. Serve your Mediterranean turkey and spinach stuffed mushrooms, a taste of Istanbul.

1 veal
chop

280

30

Lemon and Herb Grilled Veal Chops

Savor lemon and herb grilled veal chops, a tender and aromatic delight.
Chops that evoke the countryside grills of Tuscany.

Ingredients:

- 1 veal chop (6-8 oz)
- 1 tablespoon extra-virgin olive oil
- 2 cloves garlic, minced
- 1 tablespoon fresh rosemary, chopped
- 1 tablespoon fresh thyme, chopped
- Zest and juice of 1 lemon
- Salt and black pepper to taste
- Fresh thyme sprigs for garnish (optional)

Directions

1. Preheat your grill to medium-high heat.
2. Season the veal chop with salt and black pepper.
3. In a bowl, whisk together olive oil, minced garlic, chopped fresh rosemary, chopped fresh thyme, lemon zest, lemon juice, salt, and black pepper to make the marinade.
4. Brush the veal chop with the marinade.
5. Grill the veal chop for 3-4 minutes per side until it's cooked to your desired level of doneness.
6. Garnish with fresh thyme sprigs if desired.
7. Serve your lemon and herb grilled veal chop, a taste of Tuscany.

1 serving   260   40

Mediterranean Meatloaf with Feta

Indulge in Mediterranean meatloaf with a surprise of creamy feta cheese.
A meatloaf that transports you to the family dinners of Athens.

Ingredients:

- 1/2 lb ground beef
- 1/4 lb ground pork
- 1/4 cup red onion, finely chopped
- 2 cloves garlic, minced
- 1/4 cup almond flour
- 1/4 cup canned diced tomatoes (no sugar added)
- 2 tablespoons fresh parsley, chopped
- 2 tablespoons feta cheese, crumbled
- 1 teaspoon dried oregano
- 1/2 teaspoon ground cumin
- 1/4 teaspoon smoked paprika
- Salt and black pepper to taste
- Olive oil for brushing

Directions

1. Preheat your oven to 375°F (190°C).
2. In a bowl, combine ground beef, ground pork, finely chopped red onion, minced garlic, almond flour, canned diced tomatoes, chopped fresh parsley, crumbled feta cheese, dried oregano, ground cumin, smoked paprika, salt, and black pepper. Mix until well combined.
3. Form the mixture into a meatloaf shape and place it on a baking sheet lined with parchment paper.
4. Brush the meatloaf with olive oil.
5. Bake for 30-35 minutes until the meatloaf is cooked through and the top is golden.
6. Slice and serve your Mediterranean meatloaf with feta, a taste of Athens.

1 serving | 280 | 30

Greek-Style Beef and Eggplant Skillet

Enjoy a Greek-style beef and eggplant skillet, a hearty and flavorful one-pan dish.
A skillet that takes you to the family tables of Mykonos.

Ingredients:

- 1/2 lb ground beef
- 1/2 small eggplant, diced
- 1/4 cup red onion, finely chopped
- 2 cloves garlic, minced
- 1/4 cup canned diced tomatoes (no sugar added)
- 1 tablespoon fresh parsley, chopped
- 1 teaspoon dried oregano
- 1/2 teaspoon ground cinnamon
- 1/4 teaspoon ground nutmeg
- Salt and black pepper to taste
- Olive oil for cooking

Directions

1. In a skillet, heat olive oil over medium-high heat.
2. Add minced garlic and finely chopped red onion. Sauté for 2-3 minutes until they soften.
3. Add diced eggplant and cook for 5-7 minutes until it begins to brown and soften.
4. Add ground beef and cook until it's no longer pink, breaking it into crumbles.
5. Stir in canned diced tomatoes, dried oregano, ground cinnamon, ground nutmeg, salt, and black pepper. Cook for an additional 5 minutes.
6. Garnish with chopped fresh parsley.
7. Serve your Greek-style beef and eggplant skillet, a taste of Mykonos.

2 lamb chops | 280 | 25

Low-Carb Moroccan Spiced Lamb Chops

Savor low-carb Moroccan spiced lamb chops, aromatic and full of exotic flavors.
Chops that transport you to the spice markets of Marrakech.

Ingredients:

- 2 lamb chops (6-8 oz each)
- 1 tablespoon extra-virgin olive oil
- 2 cloves garlic, minced
- 1 tablespoon Moroccan spice blend (store-bought or homemade)
- Salt and black pepper to taste
- Fresh cilantro leaves for garnish (optional)

Directions

1. Season lamb chops with salt, black pepper, and the Moroccan spice blend, pressing the spices onto the meat.
2. In a skillet, heat olive oil over medium-high heat.
3. Add minced garlic and sear the lamb chops for 3-4 minutes per side until they are cooked to your desired level of doneness.
4. Garnish with fresh cilantro leaves if desired.
5. Serve your low-carb Moroccan spiced lamb chops, a taste of Marrakech.

Chapter 8:
Low-Carb Sides and Salads for Mediterranean Dining

1 serving   80   25

Mediterranean Roasted Radishes

Savor Mediterranean roasted radishes, a low-carb alternative to roasted potatoes.
A side dish that brings the warmth of the Mediterranean sun to your table.

Ingredients:

- 1 bunch radishes, halved
- 1 tablespoon extra-virgin olive oil
- 2 cloves garlic, minced
- 1 teaspoon dried rosemary
- Salt and black pepper to taste
- Fresh parsley leaves for garnish (optional)

Directions

1. Preheat your oven to 425°F (220°C).
2. In a bowl, toss radish halves with olive oil, minced garlic, dried rosemary, salt, and black pepper.
3. Spread the radishes on a baking sheet lined with parchment paper.
4. Roast for 15-20 minutes until the radishes are tender and slightly caramelized.
5. Garnish with fresh parsley leaves if desired.
6. Serve your Mediterranean roasted radishes, a taste of the Mediterranean.

1 serving   90   20

Greek-Style Grilled Zucchini

Enjoy Greek-style grilled zucchini, simple yet bursting with Mediterranean flavors.
Zucchini that takes you to the Greek islands.

Ingredients:

- 1 medium zucchini, sliced lengthwise
- 1 tablespoon extra-virgin olive oil
- 2 cloves garlic, minced
- 1 tablespoon fresh oregano, chopped
- 1 tablespoon fresh mint, chopped
- Juice of 1 lemon
- Salt and black pepper to taste

Directions

1. Preheat your grill to medium-high heat.
2. In a bowl, whisk together olive oil, minced garlic, chopped fresh oregano, chopped fresh mint, lemon juice, salt, and black pepper to make the marinade.
3. Brush the zucchini slices with the marinade.
4. Grill the zucchini slices for 2-3 minutes per side until they have grill marks and are tender.
5. Serve your Greek-style grilled zucchini, a taste of the Greek islands.

1 serving 60 15

Lemon and Garlic Sauteed Spinach

Delight in lemon and garlic sautéed spinach, a quick and healthy side dish.
A side that transports you to the sunny coast of Provence.

Ingredients:

- 4 cups fresh spinach leaves
- 1 tablespoon extra-virgin olive oil
- 2 cloves garlic, minced
- Zest and juice of 1 lemon
- Salt and black pepper to taste

Directions

1. In a large skillet, heat olive oil over medium-high heat.
2. Add minced garlic and sauté for 1-2 minutes until fragrant.
3. Add fresh spinach leaves and sauté for 2-3 minutes until they wilt.
4. Stir in lemon zest and lemon juice.
5. Season with salt and black pepper to taste.
6. Serve your lemon and garlic sautéed spinach, a taste of Provence.

1 serving | 120 | 30

Italian Grilled Eggplant with Pesto

Savor Italian grilled eggplant with pesto, a flavorful and satisfying side.
Eggplant that reminds you of the trattorias of Florence.

Ingredients:

- 1 small eggplant, sliced lengthwise
- 1 tablespoon extra-virgin olive oil
- Salt and black pepper to taste
- Pesto sauce (store-bought or homemade)
- Fresh basil leaves for garnish (optional)

Directions

1. Preheat your grill to medium-high heat.
2. Brush eggplant slices with olive oil and season with salt and black pepper.
3. Grill the eggplant slices for 2-3 minutes per side until they have grill marks and are tender.
4. Remove from the grill and let them cool slightly.
5. Serve the grilled eggplant slices drizzled with pesto sauce.
6. Garnish with fresh basil leaves if desired.
7. Serve your Italian grilled eggplant with pesto, a taste of Florence.

1 serving   120   15

Mediterranean Cucumber and Feta Salad

Enjoy Mediterranean cucumber and feta salad, a refreshing and tangy side dish.
A salad that transports you to the seaside cafes of Santorini.

Ingredients:

- 1 cucumber, sliced
- 1/4 cup feta cheese, crumbled
- 1/4 cup Kalamata olives, pitted and sliced
- 1/4 cup red onion, finely chopped
- 1 tablespoon fresh oregano, chopped
- 1 tablespoon extra-virgin olive oil
- Juice of 1 lemon
- Salt and black pepper to taste

Directions

1. In a bowl, combine cucumber slices, crumbled feta cheese, sliced Kalamata olives, finely chopped red onion, chopped fresh oregano, olive oil, lemon juice, salt, and black pepper. Toss gently to combine.
2. Chill the salad in the refrigerator for 15 minutes before serving.
3. Serve your Mediterranean cucumber and feta salad, a taste of Santorini.

1 serving   100   40

Low-Carb
Roasted
Artichokes

Indulge in low-carb roasted artichokes, tender and packed with flavor.
Artichokes that take you to the market stalls of Rome.

Ingredients:

- 2 small artichokes
- 2 tablespoons extra-virgin olive oil
- 2 cloves garlic, minced
- 1 lemon, sliced
- Salt and black pepper to taste
- Fresh parsley leaves for garnish (optional)

Directions

1. Preheat your oven to 425°F (220°C).
2. Trim the top and stem of each artichoke and remove tough outer leaves.
3. Cut each artichoke in half and scoop out the choke.
4. In a bowl, toss artichoke halves with olive oil, minced garlic, salt, and black pepper.
5. Place a lemon slice on top of each artichoke half.
6. Roast for 25-30 minutes until the artichokes are tender and slightly browned.
7. Garnish with fresh parsley leaves if desired.
8. Serve your low-carb roasted artichokes, a taste of Rome.

1 serving   90   20

Greek-Style Cauliflower Rice Pilaf

Savor Greek-style cauliflower rice pilaf, a low-carb alternative to traditional rice.
A pilaf that brings you to the family kitchens of Crete.

Ingredients:

- 1 cup cauliflower rice
- 1/4 cup red bell pepper, finely chopped
- 1/4 cup red onion, finely chopped
- 2 cloves garlic, minced
- 2 tablespoons fresh parsley, chopped
- 1 tablespoon fresh dill, chopped
- 1 tablespoon extra-virgin olive oil
- Juice of 1 lemon
- Salt and black pepper to taste

Directions

1. In a skillet, heat olive oil over medium-high heat.
2. Add minced garlic, finely chopped red bell pepper, and finely chopped red onion. Sauté for 2-3 minutes until they soften.
3. Add cauliflower rice and cook for 3-4 minutes until it's tender and slightly golden.
4. Stir in chopped fresh parsley, chopped fresh dill, lemon juice, salt, and black pepper.
5. Cook for an additional 2 minutes.
6. Serve your Greek-style cauliflower rice pilaf, a taste of Crete.

1 serving | 110 | 30

Mediterranean Brussels Sprouts with Pancetta

Delight in Mediterranean Brussels sprouts with pancetta, a flavorful side dish.
Brussels sprouts that take you to the rustic kitchens of Provence.

Ingredients:

- 1 cup Brussels sprouts, trimmed and halved
- 2 slices pancetta, chopped
- 1/4 cup red onion, finely chopped
- 1 clove garlic, minced
- 1 tablespoon fresh thyme leaves
- 1 tablespoon extra-virgin olive oil
- Salt and black pepper to taste

Directions

1. In a skillet, heat olive oil over medium-high heat.
2. Add chopped pancetta and sauté for 3-4 minutes until it becomes crispy. Remove and set aside.
3. In the same skillet, add minced garlic and finely chopped red onion. Sauté for 2-3 minutes until they soften.
4. Add Brussels sprouts halves and cook for 5-7 minutes until they are tender and slightly caramelized.
5. Stir in fresh thyme leaves, crispy pancetta, salt, and black pepper.
6. Cook for an additional 2 minutes.
7. Serve your Mediterranean Brussels sprouts with pancetta, a taste of Provence.

1 serving | 130 | 10

Low-Carb Italian Caprese Salad

Enjoy low-carb Italian Caprese salad, a classic combination of fresh flavors.
A salad that transports you to the piazzas of Naples.

Ingredients:

- 1 medium tomato, sliced
- 1/4 cup fresh mozzarella cheese, sliced
- 2 fresh basil leaves
- 1 tablespoon extra-virgin olive oil
- Balsamic glaze (store-bought or homemade)
- Salt and black pepper to taste

Directions

1. Arrange alternating slices of tomato and fresh mozzarella cheese on a plate.
2. Tuck fresh basil leaves between the slices.
3. Drizzle with extra-virgin olive oil and balsamic glaze.
4. Season with salt and black pepper to taste.
5. Serve your low-carb Italian Caprese salad, a taste of Naples.

1 serving   70   25

Lemon and Herb Grilled Portobello Mushrooms

Savor lemon and herb grilled Portobello mushrooms, a delightful side or appetizer. Mushrooms that bring you the charm of the Italian countryside.

Ingredients:

- 1 large Portobello mushroom cap
- 2 tablespoons extra-virgin olive oil
- 1 clove garlic, minced
- 1 tablespoon fresh rosemary, chopped
- 1 tablespoon fresh thyme, chopped
- Zest and juice of 1 lemon
- Salt and black pepper to taste

Directions

1. Preheat your grill to medium-high heat.
2. In a bowl, whisk together olive oil, minced garlic, chopped fresh rosemary, chopped fresh thyme, lemon zest, lemon juice, salt, and black pepper to make the marinade.
3. Brush both sides of the Portobello mushroom cap with the marinade.
4. Grill the mushroom cap for 3-4 minutes per side until it's tender and has grill marks.
5. Slice and serve your lemon and herb grilled Portobello mushroom, a taste of the Italian countryside.

Chapter 9:
Low-Carb Mediterranean Pasta Alternatives

1 serving   110   20

Zucchini Noodles with Pesto and Tomatoes

Enjoy zucchini noodles with pesto and tomatoes, a low-carb twist on classic pasta. A dish that captures the essence of the Mediterranean summer.

Ingredients:

- 1 medium zucchini, spiralized into noodles
- 2 tablespoons pesto sauce (store-bought or homemade)
- 1/2 cup cherry tomatoes, halved
- 1 tablespoon pine nuts, toasted
- Fresh basil leaves for garnish (optional)
- Parmesan cheese (optional)
- Salt and black pepper to taste

Directions

1. In a skillet, heat olive oil over medium-high heat.
2. Add zucchini noodles and sauté for 2-3 minutes until they are tender but still crisp.
3. Toss the zucchini noodles with pesto sauce.
4. Transfer to a serving plate.
5. Top with halved cherry tomatoes, toasted pine nuts, fresh basil leaves, and Parmesan cheese if desired.
6. Serve your zucchini noodles with pesto and tomatoes, a taste of the Mediterranean summer.

1 serving   120   45

Mediterranean Spaghetti Squash with Olives

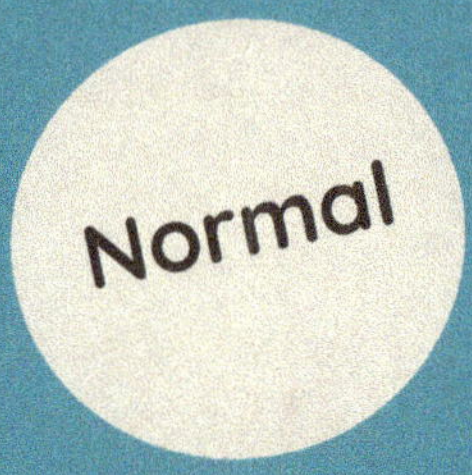

Savor Mediterranean spaghetti squash with olives, a hearty and flavorful alternative.
A dish that transports you to the coastal villages of Greece.

Ingredients:

- 1 small spaghetti squash
- 2 tablespoons extra-virgin olive oil
- 2 cloves garlic, minced
- 1/4 cup Kalamata olives, pitted and sliced
- 1/4 cup cherry tomatoes, halved
- 1 tablespoon fresh oregano, chopped
- 1 tablespoon fresh parsley, chopped
- Salt and black pepper to taste
- Feta cheese (optional)
- Lemon zest (optional)

Directions

1. Preheat your oven to 375°F (190°C).
2. Cut the spaghetti squash in half lengthwise and scoop out the seeds.
3. Brush the cut sides with olive oil and season with salt and black pepper.
4. Place the squash halves cut-side down on a baking sheet lined with parchment paper.
5. Roast for 35-40 minutes until the squash strands are tender.
6. While the squash is roasting, heat olive oil in a skillet over medium-high heat.
7. Add minced garlic and sauté for 1-2 minutes until fragrant.
8. Add sliced Kalamata olives, halved cherry tomatoes, chopped fresh oregano, and chopped fresh parsley. Cook for 3-4 minutes.
9. Use a fork to scrape the roasted spaghetti squash strands into the skillet with the olive mixture. Toss to combine.
10. Season with salt and black pepper to taste.
11. Top with crumbled feta cheese and lemon zest if desired.
12. Serve your Mediterranean spaghetti squash with olives, a taste of Greece.

1 serving | 100 | 30

Greek-Style Cabbage Noodles with Feta

Enjoy Greek-style cabbage noodles with feta, a low-carb and savory delight.
Noodles that take you to the charming villages of Crete.

Ingredients:

- 2 cups cabbage, thinly sliced
- 2 tablespoons extra-virgin olive oil
- 2 cloves garlic, minced
- 1/4 cup cherry tomatoes, halved
- 1/4 cup feta cheese, crumbled
- 1 tablespoon fresh dill, chopped
- 1 tablespoon fresh parsley, chopped
- Juice of 1 lemon
- Salt and black pepper to taste
- Lemon wedges for garnish (optional)

Directions

1. In a skillet, heat olive oil over medium-high heat.
2. Add minced garlic and thinly sliced cabbage. Sauté for 5-7 minutes until the cabbage softens and begins to caramelize.
3. Stir in halved cherry tomatoes, crumbled feta cheese, chopped fresh dill, and chopped fresh parsley.
4. Cook for an additional 2 minutes.
5. Squeeze lemon juice over the cabbage noodles and season with salt and black pepper.
6. Toss to combine.
7. Garnish with lemon wedges if desired.
8. Serve your Greek-style cabbage noodles with feta, a taste of Crete.

1 serving   180   45

Low-Carb Eggplant "Lasagna"

Indulge in low-carb eggplant "lasagna," a layered masterpiece of Mediterranean flavors. A dish that reminds you of the family kitchens in Sicily.

Ingredients:

- 1 medium eggplant, sliced lengthwise into thin strips
- 1/2 lb ground beef
- 1/4 cup red onion, finely chopped
- 2 cloves garlic, minced
- 1/4 cup canned diced tomatoes (no sugar added)
- 1/4 cup ricotta cheese
- 1/4 cup mozzarella cheese, shredded
- 2 tablespoons fresh basil, chopped
- 1 tablespoon fresh oregano, chopped
- Salt and black pepper to taste
- Olive oil for brushing
- Fresh basil leaves for garnish (optional)

Directions

1. Preheat your oven to 375°F (190°C).
2. Brush both sides of the eggplant strips with olive oil and season with salt and black pepper.
3. Place the eggplant strips on a baking sheet lined with parchment paper. Roast for 10-12 minutes until they are tender.
4. In a skillet, heat olive oil over medium-high heat.
5. Add minced garlic and finely chopped red onion. Sauté for 2-3 minutes until they soften.
6. Add ground beef and cook until it's no longer pink, breaking it into crumbles.
7. Stir in canned diced tomatoes, chopped fresh basil, and chopped fresh oregano. Cook for 5 minutes.
8. In a baking dish, layer the roasted eggplant strips, ricotta cheese, mozzarella cheese, and the ground beef mixture. Repeat the layers.
9. Bake for 20-25 minutes until the lasagna is bubbly and golden.
10. Garnish with fresh basil leaves if desired.
11. Serve your low-carb eggplant "lasagna," a taste of Sicily.

1 serving   140   35

Italian Riced Cauliflower Risotto

Savor Italian riced cauliflower risotto, a creamy and low-carb alternative.
A risotto that takes you to the charming streets of Florence.

Ingredients:

- 1 cup riced cauliflower
- 1/4 cup white onion, finely chopped
- 2 cloves garlic, minced
- 1/4 cup mushrooms, sliced
- 1/4 cup Parmesan cheese, grated
- 2 tablespoons heavy cream
- 1 tablespoon fresh parsley, chopped
- 1 tablespoon extra-virgin olive oil
- 1 tablespoon butter
- Salt and black pepper to taste
- Lemon zest (optional)

Directions

1. In a skillet, heat olive oil and butter over medium-high heat.
2. Add finely chopped white onion and minced garlic. Sauté for 2-3 minutes until they soften.
3. Stir in sliced mushrooms and cook for 5 minutes until they are tender and browned.
4. Add riced cauliflower and cook for 3-4 minutes until it's tender and begins to turn golden.
5. Reduce heat to low and stir in grated Parmesan cheese and heavy cream. Cook for 2-3 minutes until the mixture is creamy.
6. Season with salt and black pepper.
7. Garnish with chopped fresh parsley and lemon zest if desired.
8. Serve your Italian riced cauliflower risotto, a taste of Florence.

1 serving | 60 | 20

Lemon and Garlic Sautéed Broccoli Rabe

Delight in lemon and garlic sautéed broccoli rabe, a flavorful and low-carb option. Broccoli rabe that takes you to the trattorias of Naples.

Ingredients:

- 1 bunch broccoli rabe, trimmed and chopped
- 2 tablespoons extra-virgin olive oil
- 2 cloves garlic, minced
- Zest and juice of 1 lemon
- Red pepper flakes (optional)
- Salt and black pepper to taste

Directions

1. In a large skillet, heat olive oil over medium-high heat.
2. Add minced garlic and sauté for 1-2 minutes until fragrant.
3. Add chopped broccoli rabe and sauté for 5-7 minutes until it's tender and slightly crispy.
4. Stir in lemon zest, lemon juice, and red pepper flakes if desired.
5. Season with salt and black pepper to taste.
6. Serve your lemon and garlic sautéed broccoli rabe, a taste of Naples.

Substitutions

-

1 serving | 200 | 25

Mediterranean Cabbage and Beef Stir-Fry

Enjoy Mediterranean cabbage and beef stir-fry, a low-carb and savory delight.
A stir-fry that brings you the vibrant markets of Istanbul.

Ingredients:

- 1 cup cabbage, thinly sliced
- 1/2 lb ground beef
- 1/4 cup red bell pepper, thinly sliced
- 1/4 cup red onion, thinly sliced
- 2 cloves garlic, minced
- 1 tablespoon fresh parsley, chopped
- 1 tablespoon fresh mint, chopped
- 1 tablespoon extra-virgin olive oil
- Juice of 1 lemon
- Salt and black pepper to taste
- Red pepper flakes (optional)

Directions

1. In a skillet, heat olive oil over medium-high heat.
2. Add minced garlic and thinly sliced red onion. Sauté for 2-3 minutes until they soften.
3. Add ground beef and cook until it's no longer pink, breaking it into crumbles.
4. Stir in thinly sliced cabbage and thinly sliced red bell pepper. Sauté for 5-7 minutes until the vegetables are tender and the beef is browned.
5. Add chopped fresh parsley, chopped fresh mint, lemon juice, and red pepper flakes if desired.
6. Season with salt and black pepper to taste.
7. Serve your Mediterranean cabbage and beef stir-fry, a taste of Istanbul.

1 serving | 130 | 25

Low-Carb Greek Zoodle Salad

Savor low-carb Greek zoodle salad, a refreshing and zesty alternative.
A salad that takes you to the idyllic shores of Santorini.

Ingredients:

- 1 medium zucchini, spiralized into noodles
- 1/4 cup cherry tomatoes, halved
- 1/4 cup cucumber, diced
- 1/4 cup Kalamata olives, pitted and sliced
- 1/4 cup red onion, thinly sliced
- 2 tablespoons feta cheese, crumbled
- 1 tablespoon fresh oregano, chopped
- 1 tablespoon fresh parsley, chopped
- 1 tablespoon extra-virgin olive oil
- Juice of 1 lemon
- Salt and black pepper to taste

Directions

1. In a bowl, combine zucchini noodles, halved cherry tomatoes, diced cucumber, sliced Kalamata olives, thinly sliced red onion, crumbled feta cheese, chopped fresh oregano, and chopped fresh parsley.
2. In a small bowl, whisk together olive oil and lemon juice.
3. Drizzle the dressing over the salad.
4. Season with salt and black pepper to taste.
5. Toss gently to combine.
6. Serve your low-carb Greek zoodle salad, a taste of Santorini.

1 serving | 70 | 20

Mediterranean Green Bean "Pasta"

Indulge in Mediterranean green bean "pasta," a light and flavorful choice.
A dish that transports you to the countryside of Provence.

Ingredients:

- 1 cup green beans, trimmed and blanched
- 2 tablespoons extra-virgin olive oil
- 2 cloves garlic, minced
- 1/4 cup cherry tomatoes, halved
- 1/4 cup feta cheese, crumbled
- 1 tablespoon fresh basil, chopped
- 1 tablespoon fresh thyme, chopped
- Juice of 1 lemon
- Salt and black pepper to taste
- Lemon zest (optional)

Directions

1. In a skillet, heat olive oil over medium-high heat.
2. Add minced garlic and sauté for 1-2 minutes until fragrant.
3. Add blanched green beans and halved cherry tomatoes. Sauté for 3-4 minutes until the green beans are tender and slightly crispy.
4. Stir in crumbled feta cheese, chopped fresh basil, and chopped fresh thyme.
5. Squeeze lemon juice over the green bean "pasta" and season with salt and black pepper.
6. Garnish with lemon zest if desired.
7. Serve your Mediterranean green bean "pasta," a taste of Provence.

1 serving | 100 | 30

Italian Baked Parmesan Zucchini

Savor Italian baked Parmesan zucchini, a cheesy and low-carb delight.
Zucchini that takes you to the family gardens of Tuscany.

Ingredients:

- 1 medium zucchini, sliced lengthwise into thin strips
- 1/4 cup marinara sauce (no sugar added)
- 1/4 cup mozzarella cheese, shredded
- 2 tablespoons Parmesan cheese, grated
- 1 tablespoon fresh basil, chopped
- 1 tablespoon fresh oregano, chopped
- 1 tablespoon extra-virgin olive oil
- Salt and black pepper to taste

Directions

1. Preheat your oven to 375°F (190°C).
2. Brush both sides of the zucchini strips with olive oil and season with salt and black pepper.
3. Spread a thin layer of marinara sauce on each zucchini strip.
4. Sprinkle with shredded mozzarella cheese and grated Parmesan cheese.
5. Roll up the zucchini strips and place them seam-side down in a baking dish.
6. Bake for 20-25 minutes until the zucchini is tender and the cheese is bubbly and golden.
7. Garnish with chopped fresh basil and chopped fresh oregano.
8. Serve your Italian baked Parmesan zucchini, a taste of Tuscany.

Chapter 10:
Low-Carb Mediterranean Sweet Treats

1 serving   160   5

Greek Yogurt with Berries and Almonds

Savor Greek yogurt with berries and almonds, a delightful and healthy dessert.
A treat that brings you the flavors of the Greek islands.

Ingredients:

- 1/2 cup Greek yogurt
- 1/4 cup mixed berries (strawberries, blueberries, raspberries)
- 1 tablespoon almonds, sliced
- 1 teaspoon honey (optional)

Directions

1. In a serving bowl, spoon Greek yogurt.
2. Top with mixed berries and sliced almonds.
3. Drizzle with honey if desired.
4. Serve your Greek yogurt with berries and almonds, a taste of the Greek islands.

Substitutions

Honey can be substituted with maple syrup or agave syrup if desired.

1 serving

120

15

Low-Carb Dark Chocolate Bark with Nuts

Indulge in low-carb dark chocolate bark with nuts, a satisfying and guilt-free treat. A bark that brings you the joy of the Mediterranean.

Ingredients:

- 1/4 cup dark chocolate (70% cocoa or higher), melted
- 1 tablespoon almonds, chopped
- 1 tablespoon walnuts, chopped
- 1 tablespoon pistachios, chopped
- 1 tablespoon dried cranberries (no sugar added)

Directions

1. Line a baking sheet with parchment paper.
2. Pour melted dark chocolate onto the parchment paper and spread it into a thin layer.
3. Sprinkle chopped almonds, walnuts, pistachios, and dried cranberries evenly over the melted chocolate.
4. Place in the refrigerator for 10-15 minutes or until the chocolate hardens.
5. Break the chocolate bark into pieces.
6. Serve your low-carb dark chocolate bark with nuts, a taste of the Mediterranean.

Substitutions

Dried cranberries can be substituted with dried cherries or unsweetened coconut flakes if desired.

1 serving | 180 | 15

Almond and Coconut Flour Pancakes

Enjoy almond and coconut flour pancakes, a fluffy and low-carb breakfast or dessert. Pancakes that take you to the sun-drenched shores of Sicily.

Ingredients:

- 1/4 cup almond flour
- 1 tablespoon coconut flour
- 1/2 teaspoon baking powder
- 1 tablespoon Erythritol or sweetener of choice
- 1 egg
- 2 tablespoons unsweetened almond milk
- 1/2 teaspoon vanilla extract
- Butter or coconut oil for cooking
- Fresh berries for garnish (optional)
- Sugar-free maple syrup (optional)

Directions

1. In a bowl, whisk together almond flour, coconut flour, baking powder, and Erythritol.
2. In another bowl, beat the egg and stir in unsweetened almond milk and vanilla extract.
3. Combine the wet and dry ingredients and mix until you have a smooth batter.
4. Heat butter or coconut oil in a non-stick skillet over medium heat.
5. Pour a small amount of batter onto the skillet to make each pancake. Cook until bubbles form on the surface, then flip and cook the other side until golden brown.
6. Serve your almond and coconut flour pancakes with fresh berries and sugar-free maple syrup if desired.
7. Enjoy your pancakes, a taste of Sicily.

Substitutions

Erythritol can be substituted with your favorite low-carb sweetener.

1 serving   220   35

Lemon and Almond Flour Cake

Savor lemon and almond flour cake, a moist and citrusy dessert.
A cake that takes you to the lemon groves of Amalfi.

Ingredients:

- 1/4 cup almond flour
- 2 tablespoons coconut flour
- 1/2 teaspoon baking powder
- 1 egg
- 2 tablespoons Erythritol or sweetener of choice
- 2 tablespoons unsweetened almond milk
- Zest and juice of 1 lemon
- 1/2 teaspoon vanilla extract
- 1 tablespoon slivered almonds for garnish (optional)
- Lemon slices for garnish (optional)

Substitutions

Erythritol can be substituted with your favorite low-carb sweetener.

Directions

1. Preheat your oven to 350°F (175°C).
2. In a bowl, whisk together almond flour, coconut flour, and baking powder.
3. In another bowl, beat the egg and stir in Erythritol, unsweetened almond milk, lemon zest, lemon juice, and vanilla extract.
4. Combine the wet and dry ingredients and mix until you have a smooth batter.
5. Pour the batter into a greased ramekin or baking dish.
6. Sprinkle slivered almonds on top if desired.
7. Bake for 25-30 minutes until the cake is set and golden brown.
8. Garnish with lemon slices if desired.
9. Serve your lemon and almond flour cake, a taste of Amalfi.

1 serving | 210 | 15

Mediterranean Avocado Chocolate Mousse

Delight in Mediterranean avocado chocolate mousse, a creamy and guilt-free dessert. A mousse that takes you to the hidden cafes of Barcelona.

Ingredients:

- 1 ripe avocado, peeled and pitted
- 2 tablespoons unsweetened cocoa powder
- 2 tablespoons Erythritol or sweetener of choice
- 1/2 teaspoon vanilla extract
- 2 tablespoons unsweetened almond milk
- Fresh berries for garnish (optional)
- Unsweetened whipped cream (optional)

Directions

1. In a blender or food processor, combine ripe avocado, unsweetened cocoa powder, Erythritol, vanilla extract, and unsweetened almond milk.
2. Blend until the mixture is smooth and creamy.
3. Taste and adjust sweetness if needed by adding more sweetener.
4. Spoon the chocolate avocado mousse into a serving glass.
5. Garnish with fresh berries and unsweetened whipped cream if desired.
6. Serve your Mediterranean avocado chocolate mousse, a taste of Barcelona.

Substitutions

Erythritol can be substituted with your favorite low-carb sweetener.

1 serving   160   20

Keto Panna Cotta with Berry Compote

Enjoy keto panna cotta with berry compote, a creamy and elegant dessert.
A panna cotta that takes you to the romantic alleys of Venice.

Ingredients:

- 1/2 cup heavy cream
- 1/2 cup unsweetened almond milk
- 2 tablespoons Erythritol or sweetener of choice
- 1/2 teaspoon vanilla extract
- 1 teaspoon gelatin powder
- 2 tablespoons warm water
- Mixed berries (strawberries, blueberries, raspberries) for compote
- Fresh mint leaves for garnish (optional)

Substitutions

Erythritol can be substituted with your favorite low-carb sweetener.

Directions

1. In a saucepan, combine heavy cream, unsweetened almond milk, Erythritol, and vanilla extract. Heat over medium heat until it's hot but not boiling. Remove from heat.
2. In a small bowl, sprinkle gelatin powder over warm water and let it bloom for a minute.
3. Stir the gelatin mixture into the cream mixture until well combined.
4. Pour the mixture into a serving glass.
5. Refrigerate for at least 2 hours or until set.
6. Meanwhile, prepare the berry compote by heating mixed berries in a saucepan until they release their juices and thicken.
7. Spoon the berry compote over the set panna cotta.
8. Garnish with fresh mint leaves if desired.
9. Serve your keto panna cotta with berry compote, a taste of Venice.

1 serving | 130 | 30

Greek Yogurt Cheesecake Muffins

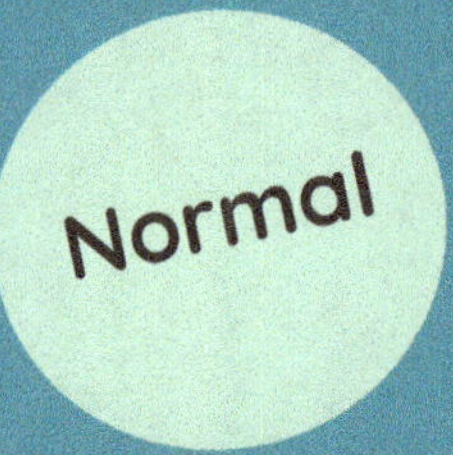

Savor Greek yogurt cheesecake muffins, a creamy and portion-controlled dessert.
A treat that takes you to the charming villages of Mykonos.

Ingredients:

- 1/2 cup Greek yogurt /n- 2 tablespoons cream cheese /n- 2 tablespoons Erythritol or sweetener of choice /n- 1/4 teaspoon vanilla extract /n- 1 egg /n- 1 tablespoon almond flour /n- 1/4 teaspoon baking powder /n- Lemon zest (optional) /n- Fresh berries for garnish (optional)

Directions

1. Preheat your oven to 350°F (175°C).
2. In a bowl, whisk together Greek yogurt, cream cheese, Erythritol, vanilla extract, and egg until smooth.
3. Stir in almond flour, baking powder, and lemon zest if desired.
4. Line a muffin tin with muffin liners and pour the batter into each cup.
5. Bake for 20-25 minutes until the muffins are set and slightly golden.
6. Garnish with fresh berries if desired.
7. Serve your Greek yogurt cheesecake muffins, a taste of Mykonos.

Substitutions

Erythritol can be substituted with your favorite low-carb sweetener.

1 serving | 110 | 25

Low-Carb Mediterranean Almond Biscotti

Indulge in low-carb Mediterranean almond biscotti, a crunchy and nutty treat.
Biscotti that takes you to the historic streets of Rome.

Ingredients:

- 1/4 cup almond flour
- 1 tablespoon coconut flour
- 1/2 teaspoon baking powder
- 2 tablespoons Erythritol or sweetener of choice
- 1 egg
- 1/2 teaspoon almond extract
- 2 tablespoons chopped almonds
- 2 tablespoons unsweetened cocoa powder (optional for chocolate biscotti)
- 1/4 teaspoon orange zest (optional)

Substitutions

Erythritol can be substituted with your favorite low-carb sweetener.

Directions

1. Preheat your oven to 325°F (160°C).
2. In a bowl, whisk together almond flour, coconut flour, baking powder, Erythritol, and chopped almonds.
3. In another bowl, beat the egg and stir in almond extract and orange zest if desired.
4. Combine the wet and dry ingredients and mix until you have a sticky dough.
5. Divide the dough in half and shape each half into a log.
6. Place the logs on a baking sheet lined with parchment paper.
7. Bake for 20-25 minutes until the logs are set and lightly golden.
8. Remove from the oven and let them cool slightly.
9. Slice the logs into biscotti and place them back on the baking sheet.
10. Bake for an additional 10-15 minutes until the biscotti are crispy.
11. Let them cool completely before serving.
12. Serve your low-carb Mediterranean almond biscotti, a taste of Rome.

1 serving   150   30

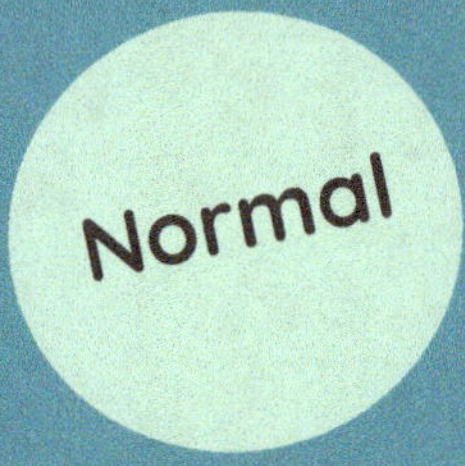

Lemon and Almond Ricotta Muffins

Enjoy lemon and almond ricotta muffins, a citrusy and moist dessert.
Muffins that take you to the picturesque coast of Sorrento.

Ingredients:

- 1/4 cup almond flour
- 2 tablespoons coconut flour
- 1/2 teaspoon baking powder
- 2 tablespoons Erythritol or sweetener of choice
- 1/4 cup ricotta cheese
- 1 egg
- Zest and juice of 1 lemon
- 1/2 teaspoon almond extract
- 1 tablespoon sliced almonds for garnish (optional)

Directions

1. Preheat your oven to 350°F (175°C).
2. In a bowl, whisk together almond flour, coconut flour, baking powder, and Erythritol.
3. In another bowl, combine ricotta cheese, egg, lemon zest, lemon juice, and almond extract.
4. Mix the wet and dry ingredients until well combined.
5. Line a muffin tin with muffin liners and pour the batter into each cup.
6. Sprinkle sliced almonds on top if desired.
7. Bake for 20-25 minutes until the muffins are set and slightly golden.
8. Serve your lemon and almond ricotta muffins, a taste of Sorrento.

Substitutions

Erythritol can be substituted with your favorite low-carb sweetener.

1 serving   210   45

Italian Low-Carb Tiramisu

Delight in Italian low-carb tiramisu, a decadent and coffee-infused dessert.
Tiramisu that takes you to the enchanting cafes of Florence.

Ingredients:

- 1/4 cup brewed espresso, cooled
- 1 tablespoon dark rum (optional)
- 1/4 cup mascarpone cheese
- 1/4 cup heavy cream
- 1 egg yolk
- 2 tablespoons Erythritol or sweetener of choice
- 1/4 teaspoon vanilla extract
- 2 low-carb ladyfinger cookies
- Unsweetened cocoa powder for dusting

Substitutions

Erythritol can be substituted with your favorite low-carb sweetener.

Directions

1. In a bowl, combine brewed espresso and dark rum if using.
2. In another bowl, whisk together mascarpone cheese, heavy cream, egg yolk, Erythritol, and vanilla extract until creamy.
3. Quickly dip each ladyfinger cookie into the espresso mixture and place them in a serving glass.
4. Spoon a layer of the mascarpone mixture over the ladyfingers.
5. Repeat the layers until you fill the glass.
6. Dust the top with unsweetened cocoa powder.
7. Refrigerate for at least 2 hours or until set.
8. Serve your Italian low-carb tiramisu, a taste of Florence.

Chapter 11:
Low-Carb Mediterranean Vegan Delights

1 serving   220   15

Mediterranean Vegan Chickpea Salad

Savor Mediterranean vegan chickpea salad, a refreshing and protein-packed dish.
A salad that takes you to the Mediterranean coast.

Ingredients:

- 1 cup canned chickpeas, drained and rinsed
- 1/2 cup cucumber, diced
- 1/2 cup cherry tomatoes, halved
- 1/4 cup red onion, finely chopped
- 1/4 cup Kalamata olives, pitted and sliced
- 1/4 cup fresh parsley, chopped
- 2 tablespoons extra-virgin olive oil
- 1 tablespoon lemon juice
- 1 teaspoon red wine vinegar
- 1/2 teaspoon dried oregano
- Salt and black pepper to taste
- Vegan feta cheese (optional)

Directions

1. In a large bowl, combine chickpeas, cucumber, cherry tomatoes, red onion, Kalamata olives, and fresh parsley.
2. In a small bowl, whisk together extra-virgin olive oil, lemon juice, red wine vinegar, dried oregano, salt, and black pepper.
3. Pour the dressing over the salad and toss to combine.
4. Crumble vegan feta cheese on top if desired.
5. Serve your Mediterranean vegan chickpea salad, a taste of the Mediterranean coast.

Substitutions

Vegan feta cheese can be substituted with crumbled tofu seasoned with nutritional yeast for a similar texture and flavor.

1 serving | 180 | 20

Italian Vegan Zucchini Noodles with Pesto

Indulge in Italian vegan zucchini noodles with pesto, a flavorful and low-carb dish. Zucchini noodles that take you to the Italian countryside.

Ingredients:

- 2 medium zucchinis, spiralized into noodles
- 1/4 cup vegan pesto
- Cherry tomatoes for garnish
- Fresh basil leaves for garnish
- Salt and black pepper to taste

Directions

1. Spiralize the zucchinis into noodles using a spiralizer or a vegetable peeler.
2. Heat a skillet over medium heat and add zucchini noodles. Cook for 2-3 minutes until slightly softened.
3. Add vegan pesto and toss to coat the noodles evenly. Cook for an additional 2 minutes.
4. Season with salt and black pepper to taste.
5. Garnish with cherry tomatoes and fresh basil leaves.
6. Serve your Italian vegan zucchini noodles with pesto, a taste of the Italian countryside.

1 serving | 180 | 35

Low-Carb Mediterranean Stuffed Bell Peppers (Vegan)

Enjoy low-carb Mediterranean stuffed bell peppers, a hearty and vegan meal.
Stuffed peppers that take you to the seaside villages of Greece.

Ingredients:

- 2 large bell peppers, halved and seeds removed
- 1 cup cauliflower rice
- 1/2 cup canned chickpeas, drained and rinsed
- 1/4 cup red onion, finely chopped
- 1/4 cup cherry tomatoes, diced
- 1/4 cup Kalamata olives, pitted and sliced
- 2 tablespoons fresh parsley, chopped
- 1 tablespoon extra-virgin olive oil
- 1 teaspoon dried oregano
- Salt and black pepper to taste
- Vegan feta cheese (optional)
- Fresh lemon wedges for garnish

Directions

1. Preheat your oven to 375°F (190°C).
2. In a large bowl, combine cauliflower rice, chickpeas, red onion, cherry tomatoes, Kalamata olives, fresh parsley, extra-virgin olive oil, dried oregano, salt, and black pepper.
3. Stuff the bell pepper halves with the mixture.
4. Place the stuffed bell peppers on a baking sheet and bake for 25-30 minutes until the peppers are tender.
5. Crumble vegan feta cheese on top if desired.
6. Serve your low-carb Mediterranean stuffed bell peppers, a taste of Greece.

Substitutions

Vegan feta cheese can be substituted with crumbled tofu seasoned with nutritional yeast for a similar texture and flavor.

1 serving | 250 | 45

Greek-Style Vegan Moussaka

Delight in Greek-style vegan moussaka, a rich and savory dish.
Moussaka that takes you to the traditional tavernas of Athens.

Ingredients:

- 2 large eggplants, sliced into rounds
- 1 cup lentils, cooked and drained
- 1/2 cup onion, finely chopped
- 1/2 cup canned diced tomatoes
- 2 cloves garlic, minced
- 1/2 teaspoon ground cinnamon
- 1/2 teaspoon dried oregano
- 2 tablespoons tomato paste
- 1/4 cup fresh parsley, chopped
- 1/4 cup extra-virgin olive oil
- Salt and black pepper to taste
- Vegan bechamel sauce (recipe below)
- Vegan parmesan cheese for garnish (optional)

Directions

1. Preheat your oven to 375°F (190°C).
2. Brush eggplant slices with olive oil and season with salt and black pepper.
3. Place eggplant slices on a baking sheet and bake for 15-20 minutes until tender.
4. In a saucepan, heat olive oil and sauté onion and garlic until translucent.
5. Add cooked lentils, diced tomatoes, ground cinnamon, dried oregano, tomato paste, salt, and black pepper. Cook for 10 minutes.
6. In a baking dish, layer half of the cooked eggplant slices.
7. Add the lentil mixture on top of the eggplant layer.
8. Add another layer of eggplant on top of the lentil mixture.
9. Pour vegan bechamel sauce over the top layer.
10. Bake for 25-30 minutes until the moussaka is golden and bubbling.
11. Garnish with vegan parmesan cheese if desired.
12. Serve your Greek-style vegan moussaka, a taste of Athens.

1 serving   240   25

Mediterranean Vegan Tofu Stir-Fry

Enjoy Mediterranean vegan tofu stir-fry, a flavorful and plant-based dish.
Stir-fry that takes you to the bustling markets of Istanbul.

Ingredients:

- 1/2 block extra-firm tofu, pressed and cubed
- 1 cup broccoli florets
- 1/2 cup bell peppers, sliced
- 1/2 cup cherry tomatoes, halved
- 1/4 cup red onion, sliced
- 1/4 cup Kalamata olives, pitted and sliced
- 2 cloves garlic, minced
- 2 tablespoons extra-virgin olive oil
- 1 tablespoon lemon juice
- 1/2 teaspoon dried oregano
- Salt and black pepper to taste
- Fresh parsley for garnish (optional)

Directions

1. In a skillet, heat extra-virgin olive oil over medium-high heat.
2. Add cubed tofu and cook until golden brown on all sides. Remove from the skillet and set aside.
3. In the same skillet, add garlic and sauté for a minute.
4. Add broccoli, bell peppers, cherry tomatoes, red onion, and Kalamata olives. Stir-fry for 5-7 minutes until the vegetables are tender.
5. Return the tofu to the skillet and add lemon juice, dried oregano, salt, and black pepper. Stir-fry for an additional 2 minutes.
6. Garnish with fresh parsley if desired.
7. Serve your Mediterranean vegan tofu stir-fry, a taste of Istanbul.

1 serving   210   40

Vegan Italian Eggplant Parmesan

Indulge in vegan Italian eggplant Parmesan, a cheesy and comforting dish.
Eggplant Parmesan that takes you to the family kitchens of Sicily.

Ingredients:

- 1 large eggplant, sliced into rounds
- 1 cup almond flour
- 1/2 cup marinara sauce (store-bought or homemade)
- 1/4 cup vegan mozzarella cheese, shredded
- 1/4 cup vegan parmesan cheese
- 1/4 teaspoon dried oregano
- 1/4 teaspoon dried basil
- Salt and black pepper to taste
- Fresh basil leaves for garnish (optional)

Directions

1. Preheat your oven to 375°F (190°C).
2. Dip eggplant slices in almond flour to coat them evenly.
3. Place eggplant slices on a baking sheet and bake for 15-20 minutes until tender.
4. In a baking dish, spread a thin layer of marinara sauce.
5. Place half of the baked eggplant slices over the sauce.
6. Top with shredded vegan mozzarella cheese, vegan parmesan cheese, dried oregano, dried basil, salt, and black pepper.
7. Repeat the layers with the remaining ingredients.
8. Bake for 20-25 minutes until the cheese is melted and bubbly.
9. Garnish with fresh basil leaves if desired.
10. Serve your vegan Italian eggplant Parmesan, a taste of Sicily.

1 serving | 190 | 30

Savor low-carb Mediterranean vegan lentil soup, a hearty and nutritious dish.
Lentil soup that takes you to the cozy cafes of Beirut.

Low-Carb Mediterranean Vegan Lentil Soup

Ingredients:

- 1/2 cup green or brown lentils, rinsed and drained
- 1/4 cup onion, finely chopped
- 1/4 cup carrots, diced
- 1/4 cup celery, diced
- 2 cloves garlic, minced
- 1/2 cup canned diced tomatoes
- 4 cups vegetable broth
- 1/2 teaspoon ground cumin
- 1/2 teaspoon ground coriander
- 1/4 teaspoon smoked paprika
- 2 tablespoons extra-virgin olive oil
- Fresh lemon juice for garnish
- Fresh parsley for garnish (optional)

Directions

1. In a large pot, heat extra-virgin olive oil over medium heat.
2. Add onion, carrots, and celery. Sauté until the vegetables are softened.
3. Add garlic, cumin, coriander, and smoked paprika. Cook for 1-2 minutes until fragrant.
4. Stir in lentils, diced tomatoes, and vegetable broth.
5. Bring the soup to a boil, then reduce heat and simmer for 20-25 minutes until the lentils are tender.
6. Season with salt and black pepper to taste.
7. Garnish with fresh lemon juice and parsley if desired.
8. Serve your low-carb Mediterranean vegan lentil soup, a taste of Beirut.

1 serving   230   45

Vegan Mediterranean Cabbage Rolls

Enjoy vegan Mediterranean cabbage rolls, a satisfying and plant-based meal.
Cabbage rolls that take you to the family gatherings of Crete.

Ingredients:

- 6 large cabbage leaves
- 1/2 cup quinoa, cooked
- 1/2 cup canned chickpeas, drained and rinsed
- 1/4 cup red onion, finely chopped
- 1/4 cup canned diced tomatoes
- 2 cloves garlic, minced
- 1/2 teaspoon dried oregano
- 1/2 teaspoon dried mint
- Salt and black pepper to taste
- 1/2 cup vegetable broth
- Vegan tzatziki sauce for serving (store-bought or homemade)
- Lemon wedges for garnish (optional)
- Fresh mint leaves for garnish (optional)

Directions

1. In a large pot, bring water to a boil. Add cabbage leaves and blanch for 2-3 minutes until softened. Drain and set aside.
2. In a bowl, combine cooked quinoa, chickpeas, red onion, diced tomatoes, garlic, dried oregano, dried mint, salt, and black pepper.
3. Place a cabbage leaf on a flat surface and trim the thick stem.
4. Spoon the quinoa mixture onto the cabbage leaf and roll it up, tucking in the sides.
5. Place the cabbage rolls in a baking dish.
6. Pour vegetable broth over the rolls.
7. Cover the dish with foil and bake for 25-30 minutes until the rolls are tender.
8. Serve the vegan Mediterranean cabbage rolls with vegan tzatziki sauce.
9. Garnish with lemon wedges and fresh mint leaves if desired.
10. Enjoy your taste of Crete.

1 serving   180   10

Italian Vegan Caprese Salad

Delight in Italian vegan Caprese salad, a simple and fresh dish.
Caprese salad that takes you to the sun-kissed gardens of Tuscany.

Ingredients:

- 1 large tomato, sliced
- 1/4 cup vegan mozzarella cheese, sliced
- Fresh basil leaves
- Extra-virgin olive oil
- Balsamic glaze
- Salt and black pepper to taste

Directions

1. Arrange tomato and vegan mozzarella cheese slices on a serving platter.
2. Tuck fresh basil leaves between the tomato and cheese slices.
3. Drizzle with extra-virgin olive oil and balsamic glaze.
4. Season with salt and black pepper to taste.
5. Serve your Italian vegan Caprese salad, a taste of Tuscany.

1 serving | 160 | 30

Mediterranean Vegan Spaghetti Squash

Indulge in Mediterranean vegan spaghetti squash, a low-carb and satisfying dish. Spaghetti squash that takes you to the charming trattorias of Naples.

Ingredients:

- 1 small spaghetti squash
- 1/2 cup canned diced tomatoes
- 1/4 cup Kalamata olives, pitted and sliced
- 2 cloves garlic, minced
- 2 tablespoons extra-virgin olive oil
- 1 teaspoon dried oregano
- Salt and black pepper to taste
- Fresh basil leaves for garnish (optional)
- Vegan parmesan cheese for garnish (optional)

Directions

1. Preheat your oven to 375°F (190°C).
2. Cut the spaghetti squash in half lengthwise and scoop out the seeds.
3. Place the squash halves on a baking sheet, cut side down. Roast for 25-30 minutes until the flesh is tender and easily shreds into spaghetti-like strands.
4. In a skillet, heat extra-virgin olive oil over medium heat.
5. Add garlic and sauté for a minute until fragrant.
6. Stir in diced tomatoes, Kalamata olives, dried oregano, salt, and black pepper. Cook for 5 minutes.
7. Use a fork to shred the roasted spaghetti squash into strands.
8. Serve the spaghetti squash topped with the Mediterranean tomato and olive sauce.
9. Garnish with fresh basil leaves and vegan parmesan cheese if desired.
10. Enjoy your Mediterranean vegan spaghetti squash, a taste of Naples.

We have a small favor to ask

We've reached the end of our culinary journey together, and we hope you've enjoyed the recipes and flavors as much as we've enjoyed sharing them with you. As we conclude this book, we'd like to ask for a small favor.

Reviews are precious to us, especially as a small publisher. They help us understand what you loved about the book and how we can improve in the future. If you can spare a moment, please consider going back to your app or the platform where you made your purchase.

Click on the review button, and if you could provide a rating and a brief sentence about your experience, we would be truly grateful. Your review could make a significant difference for us.

We want you to know that we value each and every review, and we read them all with appreciation. If you happen to notice any small mistakes, please understand that we've done our best, but errors can occasionally slip through. We hope you can overlook them and appreciate the effort we put into creating this book.

Thank you for being a part of our culinary adventure, and thank you in advance for considering our review request. Your feedback means the world to us.